silver spoon
Seasonal
DELIGHTS

Seasonal
DELIGHTS

HAMLYN

Recipes compiled by Tricia Davies

Jacket and inside photography by Vernon Morgan
Illustrations by Elaine Hill

Published in 1985 by
Hamlyn Publishing
Bridge House, London Road,
Twickenham, Middlesex, England

ISBN 0 600 32523 7

Set in 10/12 Goudy
by Servis Filmsetting Ltd, Manchester, England

Printed and bound by Graficromo s.a., Cordoba, Spain

Erratum

The pictures on pages 75 and 79
have been transposed.

Contents

Introduction

Sugar was once a luxury product nicknamed 'white gold' and found only in the homes of the very wealthy. These days we take it for granted as an essential ingredient in cooking.

Cake and biscuit recipes depend on sugar not just to sweeten but also to achieve moist, light results or a fine texture. In jams, marmalades and chutneys, sugar is a vital preservative. In yeast doughs and wine and beer-making it helps in fermentation, and in many savoury dishes it offers interesting flavour contrasts.

Silver Spoon sugars, produced from British-grown sugar beet, consist of pure natural products with no artificial colouring, flavours or added preservatives. There is a wide variety of Silver Spoon sugars for every culinary use.

Granulated Sugar Inexpensive and suitable for all sweetening purposes, granulated sugar is ideal for recipes where there is plenty of liquid and enough cooking time for the crystals to dissolve completely.

Caster Sugar Used for sifting over fruit, for cakes made by the creaming method and meringues. The sugar is an excellent decorative cooking aid as well as a super sweetener. The finer crystals are obtained by sieving granulated sugar and they dissolve more rapidly.

Icing Sugar Useful not just for icing, but also for sweetening cold drinks, fruit purées, whipped creams and ice creams. Powdered sugar dissolves instantly and is very convenient.

Preserving Sugar Specially prepared for making jams, jellies, marmalades and other preserves, this sugar has large crystals which dissolve slowly without forming a crust on the bottom of the pan.

Rich Dark Soft Sugar Adds a rich colour and flavour to cakes, puddings, biscuits and toffees. Excellent in Christmas puddings and cakes, this fine-grained sugar imparts the unique flavour of cane molasses.

Light Golden Soft Sugar Ideal for use in buttercream, shortbread and fudge, delicious with fresh stewed fruit, porridge and breakfast cereals, this is a very soft lightly molassed brown sugar.

Demerara Sugar Molassed brown sugar with large crystals, demerara is a distinctive sweetener for coffee and other hot drinks. Adds flavour and colour to cakes, biscuits, sauces, puddings and savoury dishes such as glazed ham.

Sugar Cubes Used for party drinks, ideal for taking on picnics or for tea-time, these cubes are made from granulated sugar.

Sugar Crystals for Coffee Appreciated by coffee connoisseurs, these are the largest and slowest dissolving of the brown sugar crystals; specially prepared to sweeten a cup of coffee gradually.

Golden Syrup Essential in traditional British favourites like treacle tart and syrup roly-poly, Golden Syrup imparts unique texture and flavour and is very versatile.

Black Treacle Adds a rich dark flavour to biscuits, cakes, parkin and toffees; delicious in ice-cream.

Useful Facts and Figures

Notes on metrication

In this book quantities are given in metric and Imperial measures. Exact conversion from Imperial to metric measures does not usually give very convenient working quantities and so the metric measures have been rounded off into units of 25 grams. The table below shows the recommended equivalents.

Ounces	Approx g to nearest whole figure	Recommended conversion to nearest unit of 25
1	28	25
2	57	50
3	85	75
4	113	100
5	142	150
6	170	175
7	198	200
8	227	225
9	255	250
10	283	275
11	312	300
12	340	350
13	368	375
14	396	400
15	425	425
16 (1 lb)	454	450
17	482	475
18	510	500
19	539	550
20 (1¼ lb)	567	575

Note: When converting quantities over 20 oz first add the appropriate figures in the centre column, then adjust to the nearest unit of 25. As a general guide, 1 kg (1000 g) equals 2.2 lb or about 2 lb 3 oz. This method of conversion gives good results in nearly all cases, although in certain pastry and cake recipes a more accurate conversion is necessary to produce a balanced recipe.

Liquid measures

The millilitre has been used in this book and the following table gives a few examples.

Imperial	Approx ml to nearest whole figure	Recommended ml
¼ pint	142	150 ml
½ pint	283	300 ml
¾ pint	425	450 ml
1 pint	567	600 ml
1½ pints	851	900 ml
1¾ pints	992	1000 ml (1 litre)

Spoon measures

All spoon measures given in this book are level unless otherwise stated.

Can sizes

At present, cans are marked with the exact (usually to the nearest whole number) metric equivalent of the Imperial weight of the contents, so we have followed this practice when giving can sizes.

Oven temperatures

The table below gives recommended equivalents.

	°C	°F	Gas Mark
Very cool	110	225	$\frac{1}{4}$
	120	250	$\frac{1}{2}$
Cool	140	275	1
	150	300	2
Moderate	160	325	3
	180	350	4
Moderately hot	190	375	5
	200	400	6
Hot	220	425	7
	230	450	8
Very hot	240	475	9

Notes for American and Australian users

In America the 8-fl oz measuring cup is used. In Australia metric measures are now used in conjunction with the standard 250-ml measuring cup. The Imperial pint, used in Britain and Australia, is 20 fl oz, while the American pint is 16 fl oz. It is important to remember that the Australian tablespoon differs from both the British and American tablespoons; the table below gives a comparison. The British standard tablespoon, which has been used throughout this book, holds 17.7 ml, the American 14.2 ml, and the Australian 20 ml. A teaspoon holds approximately 5 ml in all three countries.

British	American	Australian
1 teaspoon	1 teaspoon	1 teaspoon
1 tablespoon	1 tablespoon	1 tablespoon
2 tablespoons	3 tablespoons	2 tablespoons
$3\frac{1}{2}$ tablespoons	4 tablespoons	3 tablespoons
4 tablespoons	5 tablespoons	$3\frac{1}{2}$ tablespoons

An Imperial/American guide to solid and liquid measures

Solid measures

Imperial	American
1 lb butter or margarine	2 cups
1 lb flour	4 cups
1 lb granulated or caster sugar	2 cups
1 lb icing sugar	3 cups
8 oz rice	1 cup

Liquid measures

Imperial	American
$\frac{1}{4}$ pint liquid	$\frac{2}{3}$ cup liquid
$\frac{1}{2}$ pint	$1\frac{1}{4}$ cups
$\frac{3}{4}$ pint	2 cups
1 pint	$2\frac{1}{2}$ cups
$1\frac{1}{2}$ pints	$3\frac{3}{4}$ cups
2 pints	5 cups ($2\frac{1}{2}$ pints)

NOTE: WHEN MAKING ANY OF THE RECIPES IN THIS BOOK, ONLY FOLLOW ONE SET OF MEASURES AS THEY ARE NOT INTERCHANGEABLE.

Spring

In spring we turn from
the warming foods of winter
to the light, fresh foods
which are newly available.
Spring celebrations include
Valentine's Day,
Shrove Tuesday, Easter,
Burns' Night and
Mother's Day.

Spring Menu

— * —

Carrot and Orange Soup

— * —

Glazed Spring Lamb

— * —

Mandarin and Kiwi Pavlova

Carrot and Orange Soup

(Illustrated on pages 14/15)

METRIC		IMPERIAL
2	medium onions	2
450 g	carrots	1 lb
450 ml	chicken stock	$\frac{3}{4}$ pint
1	orange, finely grated rind and juice	1
1 tablespoon	granulated sugar	1 tablespoon
150 ml	double cream	$\frac{1}{4}$ pint
	salt and freshly ground black pepper	
	Garnish	
1 tablespoon	chopped parsley	1 tablespoon

Peel and roughly chop the onions and carrots and cook in the stock until just tender. Blend in a liquidiser or food processor or pass through a sieve until smooth. Add remaining ingredients. Season to taste. Reheat gently, but do not boil, otherwise the soup will curdle. Garnish with chopped parsley just before serving. **Serves 4.**

Glazed Spring Lamb

(Illustrated on pages 14/15)

METRIC		IMPERIAL
1.5-kg	leg or shoulder of lamb	$3\frac{1}{2}$-lb
	salt and pepper	
2	small sprigs rosemary	2
300 ml	light stock	$\frac{1}{2}$ pint
	Sauce and glaze	
2	oranges, grated rind and juice	2
50 g	soft brown sugar	2 oz
1 tablespoon	Worcestershire sauce	1 tablespoon
	Garnish	
	watercress and orange quarters	

Prepare the lamb for cooking. Slash the top twice and insert the rosemary sprigs. Weigh the lamb and calculate the cooking time, allowing 25–35 minutes per 450 g (1 lb) and 25–35 minutes over. Place the meat in a roasting tin and roast in a moderately hot oven (190–200 c/375–400 f/gas 5–6) for half the time.

Meanwhile, mix together the sauce ingredients and cook in a saucepan for 1–2 minutes to blend. Spoon this mixture over the lamb, replace in the oven and cook for the rest of the calculated time, basting at frequent intervals. When cooked, drain off the sauce, remove any excess fat and pour off into a saucepan. Add stock and boil together until reduced by half. Garnish the meat with watercress and orange quarters. Serve with roast or duchesse potatoes and seasonal vegetables. **Serves 6–8.**

Mandarin and Kiwi Pavlova

(Illustrated on pages 14/15)

METRIC		IMPERIAL
4	egg whites, size 2	4
175 g	caster sugar	6 oz
50 g	icing sugar, sifted	2 oz
1 teaspoon	cornflour	1 teaspoon
$\frac{1}{2}$ teaspoon	vinegar	$\frac{1}{2}$ teaspoon
$\frac{1}{2}$ teaspoon	vanilla essence	$\frac{1}{2}$ teaspoon
	Topping	
150 ml	double cream	$\frac{1}{4}$ pint
50 g	icing sugar, sifted	2 oz
2	mandarins	2
2	kiwi fruit	2

Whisk the egg whites in a large clean grease-free bowl until stiff and fluffy. Whisk in half of the caster sugar until the meringue stands in peaks. Fold in the remaining caster sugar, the sifted icing sugar, cornflour, vinegar and vanilla essence. Place on a greased 23-cm (9-in) ovenproof plate that has been lightly dusted with flour. Place in a cool oven (150 c/300 f/gas 1–2) and bake for 1 hour until firm. Turn off the oven, open the door and leave the meringue to cool.

Meanwhile, make the topping. Whisk the cream until thick then fold in the sifted icing sugar. Peel and segment the mandarins and peel and slice the kiwi fruit. Roughly chop half the fruit and fold into the cream. Spread the cream on top of the pavlova and decorate attractively with the remaining fruit slices. **Serves 5–6.**

A spoonful of sugar sprinkled over mint when it is being chopped for mint sauce will give a better flavour and make the herb easier to chop.

17

Frosted Heart Cake

(Illustrated opposite)

METRIC		IMPERIAL
225 g	butter or margarine	8 oz
225 g	soft light golden sugar	8 oz
3	eggs, size 3	3
225 g	plain flour, sifted	8 oz
	pinch of salt	
100 g	ground almonds	4 oz
100 g	dried apricots, chopped	4 oz
175 g	crystallised pineapple, chopped	6 oz
25 g	crystallised stem ginger, chopped	1 oz
	milk to mix	
	Frosting	
175 g	caster sugar	6 oz
1	egg white	1
2 tablespoons	hot water	2 tablespoons
	pinch of cream of tartar	
	pink food colouring	
	Decoration	
	frosted rose petals (see page 61)	

Cream the butter and sugar until light and fluffy, then beat in the eggs one at a time. Fold in flour, salt, ground almonds, fruits and ginger, and add enough milk to obtain a soft stiff dropping consistency. Turn the mixture into a round greased and lined 23-cm (9-in) cake tin. Place in the centre of a cool oven (150 c/ 300 f/gas 2) and bake for 3–3½ hours or until the cake is pale golden and springy to the touch. Cool; remove from tin.

Cut the cake into a heart shape by measuring 5 cm (2 in) from the top of the cake and cutting a curved U shape 19 cm (7½ in) wide (see diagram). Cut the U shape in half and put the two pieces together at the opposite end of the cake to form the point.

Make the frosting. Place all the ingredients except the food colouring in a heatproof bowl and place over a saucepan of hot water. Whisk until the mixture thickens and soft peaks form. Remove from saucepan and whisk in the food colouring. Use frosting to stick the points of the heart together and to the main cake and then cover the whole cake, spreading quickly with a palette knife to form soft peaks. Leave to set. Decorate with frosted rose petals. **Serves 10–12.**

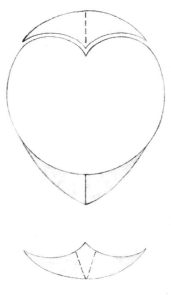

Frosted Heart Cake and Sweetheart Biscuits (page 20)

18

Sweetheart Biscuits

(Illustrated on page 19)

METRIC		IMPERIAL
75 g	butter or margarine	3 oz
25 g	icing sugar, sifted	1 oz
75 g	plain flour, sifted	3 oz
	pinch of salt	
	Glacé icing	
100 g	icing sugar, sifted	4 oz
25 g	drinking chocolate	1 oz
2 tablespoons	warm water	2 tablespoons

A cube of sugar in the biscuit tin will help to keep the biscuits fresh and crisp.

Cream fat and sugar together until light and fluffy. Add flour and salt, stir until mixture is smooth. Using a piping bag with a 1-cm (½-in) star nozzle, pipe the mixture into heart shapes on to a baking tray. Place in a moderate oven (180 c/350 f/gas 4) and bake for 8–10 minutes until pale golden brown. Cool on a wire tray.

Make the glacé icing. Mix the icing sugar and drinking chocolate in a bowl then gradually add enough of the water, stirring until smooth. Dip the heart shapes into the icing and half-coat them. Leave to dry. Tie a pretty bow round each heart with a length of red ribbon. **Makes 12–18.**

Basic Pancake Mixture

METRIC		IMPERIAL
150 ml	milk	¼ pint
150 ml	water	¼ pint
100 g	plain flour, sifted	4 oz
	pinch of salt	
1	egg, size 3, beaten	1
15 g	butter, melted	½ oz
	a little oil for frying	

Mix the milk and water together and set aside. Put the flour and salt into a mixing bowl. Make a well in the centre and add the beaten egg, half the milk and water mixture and the butter. Beat well with a wooden spoon, gradually incorporating the flour until smooth. Pour in the remaining milk and water and beat well. Heat a non-stick or seasoned frying pan with a little oil, pouring off any surplus. Pour in enough batter to thinly cover the base of the pan, and cook for about 1–2 minutes until golden brown. Toss or turn, then cook the other side. Remove and lay the pancake on damp kitchen paper. Continue to layer the pancakes and keep warm. **Makes 10.**

Variations

Wholemeal: Use wholemeal flour in place of white.
Citrus: Add the grated zest of 1 lemon, orange or lime.
Oaty: Replace 25 g (1 oz) flour with rolled oats.
Nutty: Add 15 g (½ oz) ground nuts.

Fillings

Pineapple: Mix together 100 g (4 oz) fresh chopped pineapple, 1 teaspoon ground cinnamon, 50 g (2 oz) caster sugar, 1 lemon, rind and juice, and 1 sliced banana.
Apricot: Mix together 100 g (4 oz) apricot jam and 50 g (2 oz) toasted almonds.

Bunny Spiced Loaf

METRIC		IMPERIAL
7 g	dried yeast	$\frac{1}{4}$ oz
1 teaspoon	granulated sugar	1 teaspoon
150 ml	milk, warmed	$\frac{1}{4}$ pint
350 g	strong plain flour, warmed and sifted	12 oz
1 teaspoon	salt	1 teaspoon
25 g	butter	1 oz
50 g	caster sugar	2 oz
1 teaspoon	ground mixed spice	1 teaspoon
1 teaspoon	ground cinnamon	1 teaspoon
$\frac{1}{2}$ teaspoon	ground cloves	$\frac{1}{2}$ teaspoon
100 g	sultanas	4 oz
50 g	currants	2 oz
50 g	chopped mixed peel	2 oz
1	egg, size 3	1
	Sugar glaze	
4 teaspoons	granulated sugar	4 teaspoons
4 teaspoons	cold water	4 teaspoons

Blend the yeast and granulated sugar together and add to the milk. Leave to one side until very frothy and doubled in size. Place the flour in a warmed large mixing bowl with the salt. Rub in the butter and stir in the caster sugar, spices and dried fruit. Add the yeast mixture and the egg. Knead firmly to give a soft dough, adding a little extra milk if necessary. Cover with a damp tea towel or cling film. Leave until doubled in size. Knead on to a clean, slightly floured surface. Divide the mixture up into three. Knead two pieces together, making a round ball for the body, and place on a large greased baking tray. Divide the remaining ball into two. Shape the head with one ball forming two ears. Cut off one-third of the last ball to make the feet and knead the remaining piece into a round for the tail.

Leave in a warm place until doubled in size. Place in a hot oven (220 c/425 f/gas 7) and bake for 10 minutes then lower the oven temperature to moderately hot (190 c/375 f/gas 5) for 30–35 minutes or until the dough is golden and sounds hollow when tapped. Dissolve the sugar in the water then boil. Brush the glaze over the loaf. Cool on a wire tray. **Serves 12.**

Hot Cross Buns and Marzipan Easter Eggs (both on page 24)

Hot Cross Buns

(Illustrated on page 23)

Cook's Tips

Use the basic recipe given for Bunny spiced loaf but divide into 12 balls instead of 3. Shape into rounds, place on a greased baking tray and leave to rise for 15–20 minutes. Meanwhile, knead together 25 g (1 oz) butter with 50 g (2 oz) plain flour and 4 tablespoons water. Pipe this mixture to form a cross before baking. Coat with the glaze after cooking. Place in a hot oven (220 c/425 f/gas 7) and bake for 15 minutes. **Makes 12.**

Scatter preserving sugar over fruit buns after glazing them with milk but before baking.

Marzipan Easter Eggs

(Illustrated on page 23)

METRIC		IMPERIAL
225 g	**plain or milk cooking chocolate, melted**	8 oz
	Marzipan paste	
225 g	**ground almonds**	8 oz
100 g	**icing sugar, sifted**	4 oz
100 g	**caster sugar**	4 oz
1	**egg, size 3**	1
	few drops of orange flower water	
	few drops of almond essence	

Make the marzipan paste. Knead the ingredients together until they form a pliable, but not sticky, dough. (If too sticky, knead in a little more icing sugar.) Wrap well in cling film, and keep in a cool place.

Prepare the eggs. Divide the marzipan into eight pieces. Shape each piece into an egg shape and flatten one end slightly so the egg stands upright. Skewer each egg with a long skewer or fork. Dip into the melted chocolate, and hold above the basin for a moment so any excess chocolate drops back into the bowl. Stand on cling film and allow to set. (Use any remaining chocolate either as an extra coating for the eggs or to pipe a chocolate decoration or name on them.) Leave to set. Wrap the eggs in cling film or pretty coloured foil papers. **Makes 8.**

Variation
Flatten each piece of marzipan before shaping into an egg shape. Place in the centre of each egg either 8 glacé cherries or 8 whole nuts. Continue to shape as above.

Tartan Toddy

METRIC		IMPERIAL
2	lemons, rind and juice	2
100 g	soft dark sugar	4 oz
1	cinnamon stick	1
	a pinch of ground ginger	
1	bottle Scotch whisky	1
300 ml	brandy	$\frac{1}{2}$ pint
1.75 litres	water	3 pints

Place all the ingredients in a large saucepan and heat until just boiling. Spoon into mugs and serve. **Serves 6.**

Arbroath Dessert

METRIC		IMPERIAL
1 tablespoon	oatmeal, toasted	1 tablespoon
1 tablespoon	golden syrup	1 tablespoon
2 tablespoons	whisky	2 tablespoons
600 ml	double cream	1 pint

Mix together the oatmeal, golden syrup and whisky. Whip the cream until stiff, then fold in the oatmeal mixture. Pour into individual ramekins. Chill before serving. **Serves 4–6.**

Golden syrup tastes excellent drizzled over porridge or yogurt and it makes a traditional hot sauce for steamed suet or sponge puddings.

Basic Uncooked Fondant

(Illustrated opposite)

METRIC		IMPERIAL
450 g	**icing sugar, sifted**	1 lb
2	**egg whites, size 3**	2
1 teaspoon	**lemon juice**	1 teaspoon
1 tablespoon	**liquid glucose**	1 tablespoon
	colouring and flavouring of	
	choice (see below)	

Put all the ingredients into a mixing bowl and beat well until it forms a stiff smooth dough. (If preferred, blend in a food processor or electric mixer). Sprinkle a clean surface with icing sugar and knead. Roll out into shapes or into sweet moulds. Keep in a clean polythene bag or cling film until required.
Makes 450 g/1 lb.

Colourings and flavourings
Cherry Ripes: Add 175 g (6 oz) chopped washed glacé cherries to the basic mixture. Roll into even-shaped balls.
Nutty Dates: Add 100 g (4 oz) chopped walnuts to the basic mixture. Remove the stones from 225 g (8 oz) of fresh or whole dried dates. Put the nutty fondant mixture into each date. Roll in caster sugar.
Ginger Treats: Add to the basic mixture 1 teaspoon ground ginger. Knead well. Divide the mixture into even-sized pieces and flatten. Place one small piece of crystallised ginger into each sweet. Coat in demerara sugar by rolling into little oblongs.

From the top: Peanut and Sesame Brittle, Assorted Chocolate Truffles (both on page 28) and Uncooked Fondants

Assorted Chocolate Truffles

(Illustrated on page 27)

METRIC		IMPERIAL
225 g	plain chocolate, grated	8 oz
50 g	butter	2 oz
2	egg yolks, size 3	2
25 g	icing sugar, sifted	1 oz
1 tablespoon	brandy or rum	1 tablespoon
1	egg white, size 3	1
	Coatings	
	sifted cocoa powder; coconut;	
	chocolate vermicelli; chopped	
	hazelnuts; sifted icing sugar	

Knead all ingredients except the egg white together to make a smooth stiff paste. With cold hands (dip your hands in cold water and dry well first), roll the truffle mixture into small balls about the size of a small walnut. Dip each truffle in a little beaten egg white and roll in one of the coatings. Leave to dry before packing in pretty sweet cases. **Makes 350 g (12 oz).**

Cook's Tips

A spoonful of sugar often helps to stop hiccups.

Peanut and Sesame Brittle

(Illustrated on page 27)

METRIC		IMPERIAL
450 g	soft light golden sugar	1 lb
225 g	golden syrup	8 oz
150 ml	water	$\frac{1}{4}$ pint
275 g	peanuts, salted or unsalted	10 oz
50 g	toasted sesame seeds	2 oz
15 g	butter	$\frac{1}{2}$ oz
$\frac{1}{2}$ teaspoon	bicarbonate of soda	$\frac{1}{2}$ teaspoon

Combine sugar, syrup and water in a heavy-based saucepan. Cook slowly, stirring, until the sugar dissolves. Clip a sugar thermometer to the pan and cook to 115 c/238 f. (If not using a sugar thermometer, drop a little of the syrup mixture into cold water. It should form a soft ball when gathered between finger and thumb.) Add peanuts and sesame seeds and cook to 143 c/ 289 f (or until the mixture cracks easily when a little bit is dropped into cold water), stirring constantly. Remove from heat and add butter and bicarbonate of soda. Stir to blend. Pour into a 33 x 23-cm (13 x 9-in) buttered Swiss roll tin. Leave to cool. When completely cold, break into pieces. Store in waxed paper or in an airtight tin to keep crisp. (It will keep for up to 1 month.) **Makes 900 g/2 lb.**

SWEETS

Streusel Cake

(Illustrated on page 31)

METRIC		IMPERIAL
75 g	**butter or margarine**	3 oz
175 g	**caster sugar**	6 oz
1	**egg, size 3, beaten**	1
175 g	**self-raising flour, sifted**	6 oz
	pinch of salt	
150 ml	**milk**	$\frac{1}{4}$ pint
	Topping	
75 g	**soft rich dark sugar**	3 oz
25 g	**butter, melted**	1 oz
25 g	**self-raising flour, sifted**	1 oz
1 teaspoon	**ground cinnamon**	1 teaspoon
50 g	**chopped walnuts**	2 oz

Cream the butter and caster sugar together until light and fluffy. Add the egg, flour and salt to the creamed mixture with the milk.

Make the topping. Mix the sugar with the butter and stir in the flour, cinnamon and walnuts.

Spoon half the cake mixture into a greased and lined 28 x 18-cm (11 x 7-in) Swiss roll tin, sprinkle with the remaining topping. Place in a moderate oven (180 c/350 f/gas 4) and bake for 35 minutes. Cool on a wire tray before serving. Store in an airtight tin. (It will keep for 1–2 weeks.) **Makes 12 pieces.**

29

Spicy Brandy Snaps

(Illustrated opposite)

METRIC		IMPERIAL
50 g	plain flour, sifted	2 oz
$\frac{1}{2}$ teaspoon	ground cinnamon	$\frac{1}{2}$ teaspoon
$\frac{1}{4}$ teaspoon	ground ginger	$\frac{1}{4}$ teaspoon
50 g	butter	2 oz
50 g	soft light golden sugar	2 oz
50 g	golden syrup	2 oz
1 teaspoon	lemon juice	1 teaspoon

Mix the flour with the cinnamon and ginger. Melt the butter, sugar and syrup together. Gently stir in the lemon juice and dry ingredients. Drop small spoons of mixture well apart on two greased baking trays, place in a moderate oven (160 c/325 f/gas 3) and bake for 10 minutes or until golden brown. Leave to cool for a few minutes then wrap each circle round the greased handle of a wooden spoon to shape. For a cone shape, wrap around a greased cream horn tin. Store unfilled in an airtight tin. (They will keep for 1–2 weeks.) **Makes 12.**

Granulated sugar is ideal for adding to rubbed-in cakes or those made by the melting method.

Tangy Citrus Wheel

(Illustrated on page 35)

METRIC		IMPERIAL
2	large grapefruit	2
2	large oranges	2
1 teaspoon	ground ginger	1 teaspoon
1 teaspoon	ground nutmeg	1 teaspoon
150 ml	sherry	$\frac{1}{4}$ pint
100 g	soft light golden sugar	4 oz
50 g	butter	2 oz
	Decoration	
	mint leaves	

Cut the grapefruit and oranges into halves. Remove alternate segments from each half, and replace the missing segments with a segment of the contrasting fruit. Place fruit halves on grill pan; sprinkle with ginger, nutmeg and sherry. Cover each half in soft light golden sugar and add a knob of butter. Place under a hot grill until bubbling. Serve immediately, garnished with mint leaves. **Serves 8.**

From the top: Caramel Puffs (page 32), Streusel Cake (page 29) and Spicy Brandy Snaps

Caramel Puffs

(Illustrated on page 31)

METRIC		IMPERIAL
50 g	butter or margarine	2 oz
150 ml	water	$\frac{1}{4}$ pint
65 g	plain flour, sifted	$2\frac{1}{2}$ oz
2	eggs, size 3, beaten	2
	Confectioner's custard filling	
300 ml	milk	$\frac{1}{2}$ pint
	few drops of vanilla essence	
1	egg, size 3	1
1	egg yolk, size 3	1
50 g	caster sugar	2 oz
25 g	plain flour, sifted	1 oz
	Topping	
100 g	granulated sugar	4 oz
2 tablespoons	water	2 tablespoons

Melt the butter in the water and bring to the boil. Take off the heat. Add the flour and beat well. Return to the heat and cook gently, stirring well, until the mixture forms a firm dough. Leave to cool slightly. Add the eggs gradually, beating continuously. Spoon on to a greased baking tray (allowing plenty of room to rise). Place in a moderately hot oven (190 c/375 f/gas 5) and bake for 20–25 minutes or until light golden and crisp. Make a hole in the side of each puff to allow the steam to escape. Leave to cool.

Make the custard. Heat the milk and vanilla essence until warm. Beat together the eggs and caster sugar and slowly whisk in the flour. Mix until smooth. Pour the milk on to the egg mixture. Stir well until blended together. Return to the saucepan and place over a gentle heat. Bring to the boil, whisking continuously. Cook gently for 2–3 minutes and leave to cool. Spoon or pipe this mixture into each bun. Pile the filled puffs into a pyramid.

Make the topping. Dissolve the granulated sugar in the water and bring to the boil. Clip a sugar thermometer to the pan and cook to 150c/300 f. (If not using sugar thermometer, drop a little of the syrup mixture into cold water. It should form threads that are hard and brittle.) Remove from heat and dribble the hot caramel over the pyramid. **Makes 15–20.**

A little sugar sprinkled over prepared custard or sweet milk sauces will prevent a skin from forming.

Tropical Russe

(Illustrated on page 35)

METRIC		IMPERIAL
1	packet lemon jelly	1
	(600-ml/1-pint size)	
2	firm ripe bananas	2
50 g	grapes, deseeded	2 oz
1	mango, peeled and stoned	1
26	sponge boudoir fingers	26
300 ml	milk	$\frac{1}{2}$ pint
	few drops of vanilla essence	
3	egg yolks, size 3	3
50 g	caster sugar	2 oz
150 ml	double cream, whipped	$\frac{1}{4}$ pint

Prepare the jelly as directed on the packet. Rinse a 900-ml (1$\frac{1}{2}$-pint) charlotte tin in cold water (to help prevent sticking) and pour in a little jelly to level off about 6 mm ($\frac{1}{4}$ in). Leave to set. Arrange a pattern alternating sliced banana, halved grapes and sliced mango over the jelly. Pour a little more jelly over the arranged fruit and leave to set. With a potato peeler or a sharp knife trim the sides of the sponge fingers so they fit closely together, and stand them in the tin, sugared sides towards the sides of the tin (use some crumpled-up kitchen paper to hold them in place). Warm the milk and add the essence. Cream together the egg yolks and sugar and pour on the milk, whisking well. Return to the pan and stir over the heat until the custard coats the back of a wooden spoon. Leave to cool. Whisk the partially set jelly into the double cream, then fold in the remaining fruit and custard mixture. Remove the kitchen paper and pour in a little of the mixture and leave to set. Once set add the remaining mixture and leave in the tin until firm. Keep in a refrigerator. Just before serving, trim the fingers level with the filling. Dip the base of the tin in hot water for 1 minute to loosen. Invert on to a serving plate. **Serves 6–8.**

Grapefruit Meringue Pie

(Illustrated opposite)

METRIC		IMPERIAL
	Sweet flan pastry	
350 g	plain flour, sifted	12 oz
	pinch of salt	
225 g	butter or margarine	8 oz
50 g	caster sugar	2 oz
2	egg yolks, size 3	2
	Filling	
75 g	caster sugar	3 oz
50 g	butter	2 oz
300 ml	water	$\frac{1}{2}$ pint
1	grapefruit, juice and $\frac{1}{2}$ finely grated rind	1
25 g	cornflour	1 oz
3	egg yolks, size 3	3
	Meringue	
3	egg whites, size 3	3
175 g	caster sugar	6 oz

Make the pastry. Place the flour, salt and butter in a mixing bowl. Rub in the butter. Add the sugar and mix to a stiff dough with the egg yolks. Leave to stand, covered, in a refrigerator for 30 minutes. Roll out the pastry and use to line an 18-cm (7-in) fluted flan ring. Prick the base and line with greaseproof paper and baking beans. Place in a moderately hot oven (200 c/400 f/gas 6) and bake for 15 minutes. Remove the paper and beans and allow to cool.

Make the filling. Place sugar, butter, water, grapefruit juice and rind in a saucepan. Heat until sugar has dissolved. Blend cornflour with a little water and stir into heated mixture and bring to the boil. Stir until mixture thickens. Allow to cool slightly. Beat egg yolks and add to the thickened mixture. Pour into the glazed pastry case.

Make the meringue. Whisk the egg whites in a grease-free bowl until stiff. Add half the sugar and continue whisking; fold in the remaining sugar. Cover the grapefruit mixture, place in a moderate oven (180 c/350 f/gas 4) and bake for 15–20 minutes until meringue is a light golden brown. **Serves 6.**

From the top: Tropical Russe (page 33), Grapefruit Meringue Pie and Tangy Citrus Wheel (page 30)

Nutty Banana Cake

METRIC		IMPERIAL
225 g	self-raising flour, sifted	8 oz
$\frac{1}{2}$ teaspoon	ground cinnamon	$\frac{1}{2}$ teaspoon
100 g	butter or margarine	4 oz
3	ripe bananas	3
150 g	caster sugar	5 oz
150 g	chopped walnuts	5 oz
2	eggs, size 3	2
	Decoration	
100 g	icing sugar, sifted	4 oz
1 tablespoon	orange juice	1 tablespoon
	a few walnut halves	

Put the flour and cinnamon into a bowl. Rub in the butter until the mixture forms fine breadcrumbs. Peel and mash the bananas well and quickly mix them into the flour with the remaining cake ingredients. Beat well for one minute. Turn the mixture into a greased and lined 18-cm (7-in) cake tin. Place in a moderate oven (180 c/350 f/gas 4) and bake for 40–45 minutes or until the cake is well risen and pale golden brown. Turn out and cool on a wire tray. Mix together the icing sugar and orange juice and spread over the top of the cake. Decorate with walnut halves. Store in an airtight tin for up to 1 week. **Serves 8–12.**

Chocolate Cookies

METRIC		IMPERIAL
225 g	shortbread biscuits, crushed	8 oz
75 g	icing sugar, sifted	3 oz
50 g	chopped walnuts	2 oz
100 g	butter	4 oz
50 g	golden syrup	2 oz
50 g	cocoa powder, sifted	2 oz

Put the crushed biscuits, icing sugar and nuts into a mixing bowl. Melt the butter, syrup and cocoa powder in a small saucepan. Add to the biscuit mixture and stir well. Press into a greased 18-cm (7-in) square cake tin; cool for 20–30 minutes or until set. Remove and cut into bars with a sharp knife. Store in the refrigerator covered with cling film. (They will keep for 1–2 weeks.) **Makes 12–16.**

Rub sugar cubes gently all over the skin of an orange or lemon until soaked with the oils from the zest. Crush the cubes and use in cakes, to flavour hot milk drinks or to flavour sweet sauces and custards.

Lemon and Lime Marmalade

METRIC		IMPERIAL
1.25 kg	lemons	2½ lb
1.25 kg	limes	2½ lb
3 litres	water	6 pints
3 kg	preserving sugar	6 lb

Halve the fruit, squeeze out and reserve the juice, and remove the pips. Shred the peel to the required thickness. Put the peel, juice and water into a saucepan. Tie the pips in a muslin bag and place in the pan. Bring to the boil, then simmer for about 2 hours or until the peel is tender. Remove the pips and carefully squeeze out any juice over the saucepan. Add the warmed sugar and stir until dissolved. Clip a sugar thermometer to the pan and boil rapidly until the marmalade has reached setting point (104 c/220 f). (If not using a thermometer, put some of the marmalade into a cold saucer. The surface should pucker when touched.) Remove any scum immediately and stand the marmalade to cool until a thin skin forms. Pour into warmed, sterilised jars. Lay on a wax disc and cover. Label when cold. Store in a cool dark place. **Makes approximately 10 (450-g/1-lb) jars.**

Note: Do not pour the marmalade into the jars too quickly otherwise the peel will rise to the top of the jars.

Summer

In the summer season we make the most of light salads, fresh soft fruits and cool desserts. Fruit creams, mousse and classic summer pudding are included here along with ice cream and sorbet.

Summer Menu

—— * ——

Apricot and Melon Soup
with Ratafias

—— * ——

Stuffed Bacon Chops

—— * ——

Peking Chicken

Apricot and Melon Soup

(Illustrated on pages 38/39)

METRIC		IMPERIAL
450 g	fresh ripe apricots, stoned	1 lb
1	small melon, deseeded	1
450 ml	sweet white wine, chilled	$\frac{3}{4}$ pint
150 ml	cold water	$\frac{1}{4}$ pint
75–100 g	caster sugar	3–4 oz

Place the apricots and flesh from the melon into a liquidiser or food processor with the wine, water and sugar and blend well until smooth. Chill well. Taste, adding extra sugar if required. Pour into a soup tureen. Serve with ratafias (see below). **Serves 4.**

Ratafias

METRIC		IMPERIAL
50 g	caster sugar	2 oz
50 g	ground almonds	2 oz
1	egg white, size 3	1
	few drops of almond essence	
	few sheets of rice paper	

Put the sugar, almonds, egg white and almond essence into a non-stick saucepan over a low heat. Beat together well until the mixture becomes thick and comes away from the sides of saucepan. Place the mixture in a piping bag with a 1-cm ($\frac{1}{2}$-in) plain nozzle. Line the baking tray with rice paper and pipe on 8 even-sized biscuits. Place in a cool oven (140 c/275 F/gas 1) and bake for 20–25 minutes or until set and light golden in colour. Cool on a wire tray. Remove any excess rice paper. Store in an airtight tin until required. **Makes 8.**

A spoonful of sugar
sprinkled over tomatoes
before grilling will give
them more flavour.

Stuffed Bacon Chops

(Illustrated on pages 38/39)

METRIC		IMPERIAL
4	2.5-cm (1-in) thick pork chops	4
1	onion, peeled and finely chopped	1
50 g	butter or margarine	2 oz
1 tablespoon	oil	1 tablespoon
4	sticks celery, chopped	4
1	tomato, skinned and chopped	1
50 g	fresh white breadcrumbs	2 oz
1	egg, size 3, beaten	1
	salt and pepper	
2 tablespoons	freshly chopped herbs	2 tablespoons
1	clove garlic, peeled and crushed (optional)	1

Split each pork chop, cutting nearly through the middle with a sharp knife to form a pocket.

Make the stuffing: fry the onion in half the butter and the oil until soft. Add the celery, tomato and breadcrumbs. Add the egg and season well.

Spoon the mixture evenly into the pockets in the chops. Cook on a barbecue or grill for 3–4 minutes each side, turning once. Cream the remaining butter with the herbs and garlic if using. Dot on top of each chop just before serving. **Serves 4.**

Golden Corn

(Illustrated on pages 38/39)

METRIC		IMPERIAL
4	corn cobs	4
75 g	butter	3 oz
2 tablespoons	golden syrup	2 tablespoons

Remove the husks and the silky threads from the cobs. Melt the butter with the syrup in a saucepan. Brush the cobs with the mixture. Wrap in foil. Cook on a barbecue or grill for 30–40 minutes. **Serves 4.**

Peking Chicken

(Illustrated on pages 38/39)

METRIC		IMPERIAL
8	chicken joints	8
1	small bunch spring onions, trimmed and chopped	1
4 tablespoons	golden syrup	4 tablespoons
$2\frac{1}{2}$ tablespoons	light soy sauce	$2\frac{1}{2}$ tablespoons
2	cloves garlic, peeled and crushed	2
150 ml	white wine	$\frac{1}{4}$ pint

A spoonful of sugar sprinkled over a chicken or duck before roasting will help make the skin crisp.

Trim the chicken pieces, removing any excess skin and wing tips. Place the onions and syrup in a frying pan. Add the remaining ingredients. Bring to the boil. Lower the heat, add the chicken and turn in the sauce, coating well. Cook for 30 minutes, turning once. Serve with crisp green salad or freshly cooked pasta. **Serves 4.**

Variation

This recipe is also delicious made with lamb cutlets instead of the chicken. Allow 2 cutlets per person. Pork spare ribs can also be cooked in this way; select meaty ribs and allow 225 g (8 oz) per person as a main course or 100 g (4 oz) if you are serving them as a starter.

Strawberry Soufflé with Kiwi Sauce (page 45) and Fresh Fruit Trifle (page 48)

Fruit Kebabs

(Illustrated on pages 38/39)

METRIC		IMPERIAL
2	**oranges**	2
225 g	**apricots**	8 oz
2	**bananas**	2
225 g	**cherries**	8 oz
225 g	**crisp dessert apples**	8 oz
225 g	**pears**	8 oz
225 g	**black grapes**	8 oz
225 g	**white grapes**	8 oz
50 g	**demerara sugar**	2 oz
1 teaspoon	**ground cinnamon**	1 teaspoon
100 g	**butter, melted**	4 oz
	a little icing sugar, sifted	

Prepare the fruit. Peel and segment the oranges; halve and stone the apricots; peel the bananas and cut them into chunks; stone the cherries, peel and core the apples and pears and cut them into cubes. Halve and deseed the grapes.

Prepare the glaze. Mix the sugar with the cinnamon and add to the melted butter. Thread a variety of fruits on to each skewer and brush with the butter mixture. Grill for 8–10 minutes, turning frequently during cooking to prevent burning. Just before serving, sprinkle on the icing sugar. **Serves 8–10.**

Cook's Tips

A small spoon of sugar in a vinaigrette dressing cuts the acidity of the vinegar, making the dressing smoother and improving the flavour.

Strawberry Soufflé with Kiwi Sauce

(Illustrated on page 43)

METRIC		IMPERIAL
350 g	strawberries, hulled	12 oz
25 g	granulated sugar	1 oz
3	eggs, size 3, separated	3
75 g	caster sugar	3 oz
2 tablespoons	Cointreau, orange-flavoured liqueur or fresh orange juice	2 tablespoons
3 teaspoons	powdered gelatine	3 teaspoons
3 tablespoons	hot water	3 tablespoons
300 ml	double cream, whipped	½ pint
	Decoration	
25 g	toasted desiccated coconut	1 oz
	few small whole strawberries	
	Kiwi sauce	
2	kiwi fruit	2
25 g	icing sugar, sifted	1 oz
2 tablespoons	water	2 tablespoons

Prepare the soufflé dish. Wrap a double thickness of greaseproof paper around a 13 15-cm (5–6-in) soufflé dish and tie the paper securely round it.

Make the soufflé. Blend the strawberries in a liquidiser or food processor, or press them through a sieve, with the granulated sugar. Whisk the egg yolks and caster sugar until thick and creamy, then add the Cointreau and whisk for a further 1 minute. Dissolve the gelatine in the hot water over a pan of simmering water and stir until dissolved and clear. Whisk the egg whites in a clean grease-free bowl until stiff. Fold the gelatine, egg whites, half the cream and the strawberries into the egg yolk mixture, and pour into the prepared dish. Chill until set. Remove the greaseproof paper collar by holding a damp palette knife between the paper and the soufflé, gently easing the paper away.

Decorate the sides with the coconut. Pipe the remaining cream on the top of the soufflé and top with strawberries. Make the kiwi sauce: peel the kiwi fruit and sieve or blend in a liquidiser. Add the sugar and water. Bring to the boil, cool quickly and pour over the soufflé. **Serves 4–6.**

45

Lemon Mousse

(Illustrated opposite)

METRIC		IMPERIAL
15 g	powdered gelatine	$\frac{1}{2}$ oz
3 tablespoons	hot water	3 tablespoons
50 g	caster sugar	2 oz
2	lemons, grated rind and juice	2
2	eggs, size 3, separated	2
300 ml	double cream	$\frac{1}{2}$ pint
	Decoration	
	whipped cream	
	chopped almonds	

Dissolve the gelatine in the hot water over a pan of simmering water. Put the sugar, lemon rind and juice and egg yolks into a heat-resistant mixing bowl over a saucepan of boiling water. Whisk until the mixture is light and fluffy. Whisk the cream until thick and the egg whites until they are stiff. Fold the cream into the lemon mixture, then the egg whites and gelatine. Pour into a large glass serving bowl. Leave to set in the refrigerator. Just before serving, fill a piping bag with a 2.5-cm (1-in) star nozzle with cream. Decorate with the nuts and rosettes of whipped cream. **Serves 4–6.**

*Clockwise from the top:
Loganberry and Bilberry Crush
(page 50), Lemon Mousse and
Three Fruit Chantilly Cream
(page 52)*

Fresh Fruit Trifle

(Illustrated on page 43)

METRIC		IMPERIAL
2	bananas	2
100 g	strawberries	4 oz
8	trifle sponges	8
100 g	seedless grapes	4 oz
50 g	maraschino cherries	2 oz
3	apricots	3
1	packet lemon jelly (600-ml/1-pint size)	1
450 ml	boiling water	$\frac{3}{4}$ pint
150 ml	sherry	$\frac{1}{4}$ pint
600 ml	ready-made custard	1 pint
450 ml	double cream	$\frac{3}{4}$ pint
50 g	caster sugar	2 oz
	Decoration	
50 g	flaked almonds	2 oz

Peel and slice the bananas, hull the strawberries and cut in half. Cut the trifle sponges into cubes. Arrange layers of fruit and sponge in a large glass serving bowl. Dissolve the jelly in the boiling water, as directed on the packet. Pour the sherry over the sponge and fruit. Add the jelly and chill to set. Pour over the custard. Lightly whip the cream with the sugar and spread over the custard. Chill. Decorate with flaked almonds before serving. **Serves 4–6.**

Soft Fruit Pie

METRIC		IMPERIAL
	Sweet flan pastry	
175 g	plain flour, sifted	6 oz
75 g	butter	3 oz
25 g	caster sugar	1 oz
1	egg yolk, size 3	1
	Filling	
1 kg	mixed soft fruit	2 lb
	(strawberries, raspberries	
	black, white and red currants)	
100 g	marshmallows (page 72)	4 oz
50 g	caster sugar	2 oz

Cook's Tips

Serve fruit pies topped with a spoonful of soured cream and a generous sprinkling of light golden soft sugar.

Make the pastry. Place the flour and butter in a mixing bowl. Rub in the butter. Add the sugar and mix to a stiff dough with the egg yolk.

Prepare the filling. Wash, drain and top and tail the fruit. Place the fruit and marshmallows in a shallow 20-cm (8-in) ovenproof dish.

Roll out the pastry. Cover the dish with the pastry and make a slit in the centre. Brush with water and sprinkle with the remaining sugar. Place in a moderately hot oven (200 c/400 f/ gas 6) and bake for 30–35 minutes until golden brown. Serve hot or cold. **Serves 4–6.**

Classic Summer Pudding

(Illustrated on page 51)

METRIC		IMPERIAL
7–8	medium thick slices stale white or brown bread	7–8
675–900 g	mixed soft fruit (strawberries, raspberries, loganberries, black, red and white currants, stoned red cherries)	1½–2 lb
175–225 g	caster sugar	6–8 oz
4 tablespoons	water	4 tablespoons
	double cream, to serve	

Cut off the crusts and reserve two slices of bread for the top. Use the rest to line a greased 1.15-litre (2-pint) pudding basin. Prepare the fruit. Hull the raspberries, loganberries, and strawberries. Top and tail the currants. Leave fruit whole if small or halve the larger ones. Wash the fruit, drain well and place in a saucepan with the sugar and water. Bring slowly to the boil and cook for 2–3 minutes. Remove from the heat. Place the fruit in the lined basin and top with the remaining bread. Place a saucer on top so it fits inside the rim of the basin. Put a heavy weight on top. Leave overnight in the refrigerator. To turn out, invert on to a serving plate. Serve topped with piped whipped cream. **Serves 6–8.**

Apricot Charlotte

(Illustrated opposite)

METRIC		IMPERIAL
150 g	butter	5 oz
8–9	slices wholemeal bread,	8–9
	crusts removed	
350 g	dried apricots	12 oz
1	lemon, grated rind and juice	1
300 ml	water	$\frac{1}{2}$ pint
100 g	soft rich dark sugar	4 oz
25 g	flaked almonds	1 oz
	ice-cream or custard, to serve	

Before baking, fill cooking apples with a mixture of demerara sugar, butter and raisins or chopped dried apricots.

Melt the butter and dip in the slices of bread. Line a 1-litre (1¾-pint) ovenproof dish with bread, leaving some for the top. Stew the apricots with the lemon juice, rind and water. When half-cooked, layer the fruit in the dish with three-quarters of the brown sugar and the almonds in the dish. Cover with the remaining bread, sprinkle on the remaining sugar and any extra butter. Place in a moderately hot oven (200 c/400 f/gas 6) and bake until crisp. Serve hot with ice cream or custard. **Serves 6.**

Loganberry and Bilberry Crush

(Illustrated on page 47)

METRIC		IMPERIAL
350 g	loganberries, thawed if frozen	12 oz
100 g	bilberries, thawed if frozen	4 oz
	caster sugar to taste	
900 ml	double cream, lightly whipped	1½ pints

If using fresh fruit, hull the loganberries and top and tail the bilberries, wash the fruit well, and drain. Divide the fruit into three portions. Place a layer in a glass dish with a little sugar. Cover the fruit with one third of the cream. Continue to layer the fruit, sugar and cream, finishing with cream. Chill. Just before serving, stir to create a marbled effect. **Serves 4–6.**

Note: This recipe is good for any soft fruit of the season or fruit that has been frozen and 'bleeds' a lot when thawed.

Classic Summer Pudding (page 49) and Apricot Charlotte

Three Fruit Chantilly Cream

(Illustrated on page 47)

METRIC		IMPERIAL
450 g	redcurrants, thawed if frozen	1 lb
450 g	raspberries, thawed if frozen	1 lb
250 g	blackcurrants, thawed if frozen	9 oz
750 ml	water	$1\frac{1}{4}$ pints
100 g	granulated sugar	4 oz
50–60 g	cornflour	2–$2\frac{1}{2}$ oz
	Chantilly cream	
150 ml	double cream	$\frac{1}{4}$ pint
2 tablespoons	iced water	2 tablespoons
2 teaspoons	icing sugar, sifted	2 teaspoons
2	drops vanilla essence	2

Fill the centre of pear halves – ripe fresh fruit or drained canned pears – with light golden soft sugar and a knob of butter. Grill until bubbling.

If using fresh fruit, top and tail, wash and drain. Cook 250 g/9 oz each of redcurrants, raspberries and blackcurrants together with the water and sugar until soft. Pass through a sieve or blend for a short time in a liquidiser or food processor. Blend the cornflour with a little of the fruit purée then add this to the rest of the purée. Heat in a saucepan until it thickens. Allow to cool until lukewarm and fold in the remaining whole fruit. Pour into eight serving dishes and chill well.

Make the Chantilly cream. Place all ingredients into a bowl and whisk until cream has thickened to form soft peaks. Decorate the fruit with piped Chantilly cream before serving. **Serves 8.**

Mango Fool

(Illustrated on page 55)

METRIC		IMPERIAL
2	ripe mangoes	2
300 ml	double cream	$\frac{1}{2}$ pint
1–3 tablespoons	golden syrup	1–3 tablespoons

Peel and stone the mangoes. Place the fruit, cream and syrup into a liquidiser or food processor. Blend for 30 seconds or until thoroughly mixed. Pour into six individual dishes. Chill for 1 hour before serving. **Serves 6.**

Dutch Apple Cake

METRIC		IMPERIAL
100 g	butter	4 oz
225 g	self-raising flour, sifted	8 oz
100 g	granulated sugar	4 oz
1	egg, size 3, beaten	1
2–3 tablespoons	milk	2–3 tablespoons
4	dessert apples	4
	Topping	
50 g	butter	2 oz
50 g	soft light golden sugar	2 oz
	whipped cream, to serve	

Rub the butter into the flour until it resembles fine breadcrumbs, add the granulated sugar and mix to a soft dough with the egg and a little milk. Put into a lined 23 × 33-cm (9 × 13-in) Swiss roll tin and level the top. Core the dessert apples and cut into thin slices. Arrange on the mixture in layers.

Make the topping. Melt the butter and sugar together and pour over the apples. Bake in a moderate oven (180 c/350 f/gas 4) and bake for 1 hour or until firm to the touch. Serve cold with whipped cream. **Serves 8–10.**

Put three or four cubes of sugar in a suitcase before storing it away for any length of time; this will prevent the case from smelling musty and damp.

Almond Biscuits

METRIC		IMPERIAL
75 g	caster sugar	3 oz
25 g	ground almonds	1 oz
1	egg, size 3	1
65 g	plain flour, sifted	2½ oz
	pinch of salt	
1½ tablespoons	single cream	1½ tablespoons

Cream together the sugar, almonds and the egg, then stir in the flour and salt until the mixture is smooth. Leave to stand for 30 minutes in the refrigerator. Add the cream. Spread the mixture thinly into 10-cm (4-in) circles on a greased baking sheet. Place in a moderate oven (180 c/350 f/gas 4) and cook for 3–4 minutes. While still warm, the biscuits can be shaped around the handle of a wooden spoon.

Peach Sorbet

(Illustrated opposite)

METRIC		IMPERIAL
100 g	caster sugar	4 oz
4 tablespoons	water	4 tablespoons
1 tablespoon	lemon juice	1 tablespoon
4	ripe peaches, skinned, stoned and puréed	4
2	egg whites, size 3	2

Dissolve the sugar in the water and boil until syrupy. Add the lemon juice, and whisk the mixture into the peach purée. Put in the freezer until half-frozen. Whisk the egg whites until stiff. Whisk the partly frozen mixture, then fold in the egg whites. Freeze, whisking once again before completely frozen. Use as required. **Serves 4–6.**

Nectarine Cream

(Illustrated opposite)

METRIC		IMPERIAL
2	nectarines	2
175 ml	plain yogurt	6 fl oz
40 g	icing sugar, sifted	1½ oz
1 tablespoon	powdered gelatine	1 tablespoon
	juice of ½ orange	
150 ml	double cream	¼ pint
	Decoration	
	whipped cream	

Blanch the nectarines and remove the skins and stones. Purée the fruit in a liquidiser or food processor with the yogurt and icing sugar. Dissolve the gelatine in the warmed orange juice and stir it, still warm, into the nectarine and cream mixture. Chill for 5 minutes then whip the cream stiffly and fold into the fruit mixture. Divide the mixture between six 100–200-ml (6–7-fl oz) moulds and leave to set for 2–3 hours in the refrigerator.

To serve, dip the moulds up to the rim in hot water for a few seconds and then turn them on to individual plates. Decorate with whipped cream. **Serves 6.**

Clockwise from top right: Mango Fool (page 52), Peach Sorbet and Nectarine Cream

Grand Marnier Citrus Cake

METRIC		IMPERIAL
100 g	caster sugar	4 oz
100 g	butter	4 oz
2	eggs, size 3, beaten	2
100 g	self-raising flour, sifted	4 oz
	Syrup	
2	oranges	2
1	lemon	1
50 g	caster sugar	2 oz
2 tablespoons	Grand Marnier or	2 tablespoons
	orange-flavoured liqueur	
	whipped cream, to serve	

Cream together the sugar and butter until pale and creamy. Gradually add the beaten eggs, then fold the flour into the creamed mixture. Pour into a greased 20-cm (8-in) round sandwich tin. Place in a moderately hot oven (190 c/375 f/gas 5) and bake for 20 minutes or until springy to the touch. Remove from the oven and allow to cool in the tin.

To make the syrup, squeeze the juice from the oranges and lemon. Put the fruit juice and sugar into a saucepan. Boil until syrupy, then add the Grand Marnier. Pour over the cake and leave covered, in the refrigerator, for 2 days before serving. Serve with whipped cream. Store in an airtight tin for 1–2 days. **Serves 8.**

Rich Cornish Ice

METRIC		IMPERIAL
300 ml	milk	½ pint
75 g	caster sugar	3 oz
2	egg yolks, size 3	2
1	egg, size 3	1
150 ml	rich clotted cream	¼ pint
½ teaspoon	vanilla essence	½ teaspoon
150 ml	whipping cream,	¼ pint
	lightly whipped	

Whisk together the milk, sugar, egg yolks and egg. Cook in a double saucepan or in a bowl over hot water, stirring all the time until the mixture is thick and coats the back of a wooden spoon.

Stir in the clotted cream, vanilla essence and the whipped cream. Pour into a bowl. Freeze until half-frozen. Remove from the freezer and beat well. Return to the freezer until completely frozen. (For a lighter ice cream fold in the two whisked egg whites after removing from the freezer the first time.) **Makes 900 ml (1½ pints).**

Variations

Fruity Themes: After removing the ice cream from the freezer the first time add 75 g–100 g (3–4 oz) lightly chopped fruit such as strawberries, raspberries, peaches or plums.

Nutty Ways: Add 50 g–75 g (2–3 oz) chopped toasted nuts such as walnuts, hazelnuts and pistachio nuts.

Crisp Cherry Pie

(Illustrated on page 59)

METRIC		IMPERIAL
175 g	soft margarine or butter	6 oz
250 g	plain flour, sifted	9 oz
2 tablespoons	cold water	2 tablespoons
	Filling and glaze	
675 g	ripe cherries, stoned and washed	1½ lb
100 g	granulated sugar	4 oz
	a little beaten egg	
1 tablespoon	desiccated coconut	1 tablespoon
1 teaspoon	caster sugar	1 teaspoon
	custard or ice cream, to serve	

Rub the margarine into the flour, add water, and stir to form a stiff dough. Turn on to a floured surface and knead to form a smooth but firm dough. Cover with cling film and leave to stand for 30 minutes in the refrigerator.

Place cherries in a 600-ml (1-pint) pie dish, sprinkle over the granulated sugar. Roll out the pastry and cover the pie dish. Trim the pastry and flute the edges. Brush with beaten egg and sprinkle with the coconut and caster sugar mixed together. Place in a moderately hot oven (200 c/400 f/gas 6) and bake for 20 minutes then lower the temperature to moderate (180 c/350 f/gas 4) and cook for a further 20 minutes until golden brown. Serve hot or cold with custard or ice cream. **Serves 4–6.**

Redcurrant Cheesecake

(Illustrated opposite)

METRIC		IMPERIAL
100 g	digestive biscuits	4 oz
150 g	caster sugar	5 oz
50 g	butter, melted	2 oz
350 g	redcurrants	12 oz
2 tablespoons	water	2 tablespoons
2	eggs, size 3, separated	2
$\frac{1}{2}$ teaspoon	vanilla essence	$\frac{1}{2}$ teaspoon
15 g	powdered gelatine	$\frac{1}{2}$ oz
6 tablespoons	hot water	6 tablespoons
225 g	cream cheese	8 oz
150 ml	double cream	$\frac{1}{4}$ pint
25 g	chopped nuts	1 oz

A spoonful of sugar and a knob of fat rubbed well into very dry or stained hands (for example after picking blackberries) will clean and soften the skin. When the hands have been thoroughly massaged together, wash off the sugar and fat in warm soapy water. Repeat if the stains are very bad.

Crush the biscuits and mix with 50 g (2 oz) of the sugar and the melted butter. Press the mixture into the base of a loose-based 18-cm (7-in) cake tin with the back of a damp metal spoon. Cook the redcurrants in the water until soft. Pass through a sieve to make a purée or blend in a liquidiser or food processor. Beat the egg yolks and remaining sugar together until creamy. Add the vanilla essence. Dissolve the gelatine in the hot water over a pan of simmering water. Add the cheese and fruit purée to the egg yolks. Mix in the gelatine and leave in the refrigerator until beginning to set. Whip the egg whites until stiff. Fold the cream and egg whites into the mixture and pour into the cake tin. Leave to set. Decorate with chopped nuts before serving.
Serves 6–8.

Variations
This recipe is delicious with other types of cooked soft fruit.

Redcurrant Cheesecake and Crisp Cherry Pie (page 57)

Danish Pastries

METRIC		IMPERIAL
1 teaspoon	caster sugar	1 teaspoon
450 ml	warm milk or water	$\frac{3}{4}$ pint
15 g	dried yeast	$\frac{1}{2}$ oz
575 g	strong plain flour, sifted	$1\frac{1}{4}$ lb
	pinch of salt	
40 g	melted butter	$1\frac{1}{2}$ oz
225 g	butter	8 oz
	a little beaten egg	
6	glacé cherries	6
	a little glacé icing	
	Almond paste filling	
15 g	butter	$\frac{1}{2}$ oz
75 g	caster sugar	3 oz
75 g	ground almonds	3 oz
2–3	drops almond essence	2–3
	a little beaten egg	
	Apple filling	
2	eating apples	2
	a little lemon juice	
25 g	soft brown sugar	1 oz
3–4 tablespoons	apricot jam	3–4 tablespoons

Glacé icing is easy to make. Mix sifted icing sugar with a little warm water to make a smooth, thick icing. Flavour and colour as required.

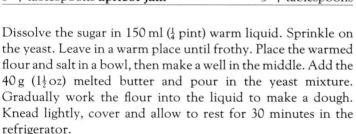

Dissolve the sugar in 150 ml ($\frac{1}{4}$ pint) warm liquid. Sprinkle on the yeast. Leave in a warm place until frothy. Place the warmed flour and salt in a bowl, then make a well in the middle. Add the 40 g ($1\frac{1}{2}$ oz) melted butter and pour in the yeast mixture. Gradually work the flour into the liquid to make a dough. Knead lightly, cover and allow to rest for 30 minutes in the refrigerator.

Soften the remaining butter and divide into three. Roll out the dough to an oblong 64 × 18 cm (27 × 7 in). Dot one portion of softened butter over the top two-thirds of the dough. Fold the unbuttered third over half the fat and the buttered third over the top of that. Press all the edges together to seal well. Cover and leave to stand for 20 minutes in the refrigerator. Continue and repeat the rolling and folding process until all the fat is used up. Then roll and fold the dough twice more. Chill well while making the fillings.

Make the fillings. Mix all the ingredients together for the almond filling adding just enough beaten egg to make a firm paste. For the apple filling, peel, core and slice the apples sprinkle with the lemon juice and mix with the remaining ingredients.

Divide the dough into three. Keep two-thirds chilled while

you are working on the last portion. One by one, roll out each third to a 25-cm (10-in) square and cut into four. Fill each square with a little of one of the fillings. Press the points of each square to the centre over the filling and stick together with a little egg. Top the middle with a glacé cherry if liked. Place the prepared pastries on to a greased baking tray and leave for 20–30 minutes in a warm place to rise. Place in a hot oven (220 c/425 f/gas 7) and bake for about 10 minutes until risen and golden. While still hot, brush with a little glacé icing, then transfer to a wire tray to cool. The pastries are best eaten on the same day they are made or they can be frozen before the glacé icing is added. **Makes 15–16.**

Frosted Fruit, Petals and Leaves

These are a lovely way to decorate a cake, dessert or drink. Once they are made they can be stored up to 1 month in an airtight box layered with tissue. When preparing the petals do make sure they are edible and clean. If in doubt, ask an expert. Collect together any fresh flower petals and some leaves, such as rose petals, violets, carnations, forget-me-not, fruit blossoms, prim-roses, mint leaves or herbs.

Using a small clean art paintbrush, paint the flowers with a little beaten egg white whisked with 1 teaspoon cold water. Do this carefully front and back of the petals and leaves making sure that they are all covered. Dredge lightly with caster sugar. Lay on a wire tray to dry in a warm place. Turn once or twice to prevent them sticking.

Washed and dried fruit like grapes, cherries and soft fruit, etc, can be treated as above but they must be used within 24 hours.

Autumn

Autumn is the harvest
season when we
preserve the fruits and
vegetables in jams and jellies,
chutneys and pickles.
As the nights draw in we
celebrate Halloween and
Bonfire Night.

Autumn Menu

— * —

Sweet and Sour Prawns

— * —

Autumn Gold Chicken

*

Crème Brûlée

Sweet and Sour Prawns

(Illustrated on pages 62/63)

METRIC		IMPERIAL
350 g	peeled prawns, thawed if frozen	12 oz
1 tablespoon	cornflour	1 tablespoon
4 tablespoons	vegetable oil	4 tablespoons
	Sauce	
1 tablespoon	cornflour	1 tablespoon
2 tablespoons	soft light golden sugar	2 tablespoons
2 tablespoons	wine vinegar	2 tablespoons
2 tablespoons	orange juice	2 tablespoons
1 tablespoon	soy sauce	1 tablespoon
1 tablespoon	concentrated tomato purée	1 tablespoon
6 tablespoons	water	6 tablespoons

Mix all the sauce ingredients together. Toss the prawns in the cornflour. Heat the oil in a frying-pan, and fry the prawns for 2–3 minutes. Add the sauce mixture and cook, stirring continuously, until sauce thickens. Serve immediately. **Serves 6.**

Autumn Gold Chicken

(Illustrated on pages 62/63)

METRIC		IMPERIAL
1.5 kg	roasting chicken	3½ lb
2 tablespoons	golden syrup	2 tablespoons
1 tablespoon	soy sauce	1 tablespoon
300 ml	chicken stock	½ pint
2 tablespoons	vinegar	2 tablespoons
1 tablespoon	cornflour	1 tablespoon
50 g	dried dates, stoned and halved	2 oz
1	yellow pepper, cored, deseeded and cut into strips	1
1 tablespoon	fresh root ginger, peeled and chopped	1 tablespoon

Place the chicken in a moderately hot oven (190 c/375 f/gas 5) and roast for 1 hour. Blend the syrup, soy sauce, stock, vinegar and cornflour in a pan. Bring to the boil and stir well, add the dates, peppers and ginger. Simmer for 10 minutes – pour the sauce over the chicken and return to the oven for a further 30 minutes until the chicken is cooked. Serve with long-grain rice and seasonal vegetables. **Serves 6.**

Crème Brûlée

(Illustrated on pages 62/63)

METRIC		IMPERIAL
2	eggs, size 3	2
2	egg yolks, size 3	2
300 ml	double cream	$\frac{1}{2}$ pint
300 ml	single cream	$\frac{1}{2}$ pint
75 g	caster sugar	3 oz
1 teaspoon	vanilla essence	1 teaspoon

Beat the eggs and yolks together in a bowl. In a saucepan, heat the double and single cream gently until the mixture is just warm. Pour on to the eggs. Add 25 g (1 oz) sugar and the vanilla essence. Strain the mixture into four ramekins. Place in a double saucepan or a roasting tin standing in 2.5 cm (1 in) of water in a moderate oven (160 c/325 f/gas 3) and cook for 20–30 minutes. Leave until cold. Sprinkle the remaining sugar on the surface and grill until caramelised. Chill. Just before serving, crack the caramel with the back of a metal spoon. **Serves 4.**

Variations
Fruit Brûlée: Put a layer of fresh fruit on the bottom of the dish, for example 150 g (5 oz) cooked apples, strawberries, raspberries.
Quick Brûlée: Fold 150 ml ($\frac{1}{4}$ pint) slightly whipped cream into 600 ml (1 pint) ready-made custard. Sprinkle on the 75 g (3 oz) caster sugar and continue as above.

A little black treacle can be added to enrich barbecue sauces, home-made chutneys or mincemeat.

Pumpkin Pie

(Illustrated opposite)

METRIC		IMPERIAL
225 g	shortcrust pastry	8 oz
	(see Treacle tart, page 68)	
450 g	cooked pumpkin flesh, puréed	1 lb
	or one can pumpkin, drained	
	and puréed	
1 teaspoon	ground cinnamon	1 teaspoon
$\frac{1}{2}$ teaspoon	ground ginger	$\frac{1}{2}$ teaspoon
$\frac{1}{2}$ teaspoon	ground nutmeg	$\frac{1}{2}$ teaspoon
$\frac{1}{2}$ teaspoon	salt	$\frac{1}{2}$ teaspoon
75 g	soft light golden sugar	3 oz
3	eggs, size 3	3
150 ml	single cream	$\frac{1}{4}$ pint

Roll out the pastry and use to line a 20-cm (8-in) pie plate or flan ring. Prick the base and line with greaseproof paper and baking beans. Glaze the pastry with a little milk and sugar. Place in a moderately hot oven (190 c/375 f/gas 5) and bake for 15–20 minutes. Remove the paper and beans. Meanwhile, prepare the filling by mixing all the ingredients together. Pour into the pastry case and bake at the above temperature for a further 40–45 minutes. Serve with freshly whipped cream flavoured with a little ground cinnamon and caster sugar. Serve hot or cold. **Serves 4–6.**

Note: To make a fun Halloween lantern, scoop the flesh carefully out of the pumpkin. Cut out eyes, nose and a mouth and place in a couple of lit candles. When scooping out the flesh discard the seeds, chop into pieces and cook. Serve as a delicious vegetable (like marrow) or make into a purée for soups or pie fillings.

Clockwise from the top: Parkin (page 69), Toffee Apples and Treacle Tart (both on page 68), and Pumpkin Pie

Toffee Apples

(Illustrated on page 67)

METRIC		IMPERIAL
8	**medium dessert apples**	8
450 g	**granulated sugar**	1 lb
50 g	**butter**	2 oz
1 tablespoon	**vinegar**	1 tablespoon
150 ml	**water**	$\frac{1}{4}$ pint
1 tablespoon	**golden syrup**	1 tablespoon

Wipe the apples and push a lollipop stick into each core. Place all the other ingredients in a saucepan and cook over a gentle heat until the sugar is dissolved, then clip a sugar thermometer to the pan and boil to 145 c/290 f. (If not using a thermometer, drop a little of the mixture into cold water. It should break easily when touched.) Dip the apples into the toffee, shake off excess. Leave to cool on a buttered plate. When cold, wrap each apple in cellophane or cling film. **Makes 8.**

Note: For an extra special treat dip half the coated apples into melted chocolate. Or, for a crunchy finish, after removing the excess toffee, dip the apples into demerara sugar.

Treacle Tart

(Illustrated on page 67)

METRIC		IMPERIAL
	Shortcrust pastry	
225 g	**plain or wholemeal flour, sifted**	8 oz
	pinch of salt	
50 g	**lard**	2 oz
50 g	**margarine**	2 oz
	cold water	
	Filling	
350 g	**golden syrup**	12 oz
50 g	**brown breadcrumbs**	2 oz
$\frac{1}{2}$	**orange, grated rind only**	$\frac{1}{2}$

Place the flour and salt in a bowl, rub in the lard and margarine until the mixture resembles fine breadcrumbs. Mix to a soft dough using cold water. Roll out the pastry and use to line a 25-cm (10-in) ovenproof plate. Re-roll the trimmings, cut into 12-mm ($\frac{1}{2}$-in) strips, and reserve for decoration.

Make the filling. Mix the syrup, breadcrumbs and orange rind together. Pour filling on to plate. Decorate in a lattice design with strips of pastry. Place in a moderately hot oven (200 c/400 f/gas 6) and bake for 30 minutes. **Serves 6.**

Parkin

(Illustrated on page 67)

METRIC		IMPERIAL
175 g	**plain flour, sifted**	6 oz
1 teaspoon	**ground cinnamon**	1 teaspoon
2 teaspoons	**ground ginger**	2 teaspoons
1 teaspoon	**bicarbonate of soda**	1 teaspoon
175 g	**medium oatmeal**	6 oz
75 g	**margarine**	3 oz
50 g	**soft light golden sugar**	2 oz
225 g	**black treacle**	8 oz
1	**egg, size 3**	1
1$\frac{1}{2}$ tablespoons	**milk**	1$\frac{1}{2}$ tablespoons

Mix all the dry ingredients together. Warm the margarine, sugar and treacle together until the margarine has melted and the sugar dissolved. Beat the egg with the milk and add the liquids to the dry ingredients, stir well. Pour into a greased and lined 20-cm (8-in) square cake tin, place in a moderate oven (160 c/325 f/gas 3) and bake for 55–65 minutes. Cut into squares when cold. Store in an airtight tin. (It will keep for 2–3 weeks.) **Makes 12–14 squares.**

Make cinnamon butter for spreading on slices of teabread, hot toast or toasted crumpets. Beat light golden soft sugar and ground cinnamon into butter until creamy, then chill before using.

Treacle Toffee

(Illustrated opposite)

METRIC		IMPERIAL
450 g	soft light golden sugar	1 lb
150 ml	water	$\frac{1}{4}$ pint
	pinch of cream of tartar	
75 g	butter	3 oz
225 g	black treacle	8 oz

Put all the ingredients into a large saucepan and heat slowly until sugar is dissolved. Clip a sugar thermometer to the pan and boil briskly, without stirring, to 132 c/270 f. (If not using a thermometer, drop a little of the mixture into cold water. It should break easily when touched.) Pour into a greased 28 × 18-cm (11 × 7-in) Swiss roll tin and mark into squares. Break into squares when cold and store, wrapped in cling film, in an airtight tin. (It will keep for 1–2 weeks.) **Makes 60–70 pieces.**

Barbecued Bananas

(Illustrated opposite)

METRIC		IMPERIAL
4	bananas, just ripe	4
2 tablespoons	golden syrup	2 tablespoons
$\frac{1}{2}$	lemon, juice only	$\frac{1}{2}$
50 g	soft brown sugar	2 oz

Carefully cut the bananas lengthways with the skins on. Ease the two halves apart and spread the golden syrup on each half, sprinkle with lemon juice and soft brown sugar. Press the bananas together and wrap loosely in foil. Cook on a barbecue or under a grill for 5–8 minutes. **Serves 4.**

From the top: Treacle Toffee, Barbecued Bananas and Toasted Marshmallows with Raspberry Sauce (page 72)

Marshmallows

METRIC		IMPERIAL
275 g	granulated sugar or	10 oz
	sugar cubes	
150 ml	cold water	$\frac{1}{4}$ pint
1	lemon, strained juice of	1
1 tablespoon	golden syrup	1 tablespoon
2 tablespoons	powdered gelatine	2 tablespoons
4 tablespoons	hot water	4 tablespoons
1	egg white, stiffly beaten	1
	flavour and colouring	
	a little icing sugar,	
	chopped nuts, desiccated	
	coconut or other coating	

Put the sugar, cold water, lemon juice and golden syrup into a heavy-based saucepan. Dissolve the sugar then clip a sugar thermometer to the pan and boil to 130 c/260 F. Dissolve the gelatine in the hot water over a pan of simmering water. Remove the sugar syrup from the heat and pour on to the gelatine, stirring well. Pour the mixture onto the egg white in a slow stream, whisking all the time with an electric mixer. Continue whisking until very thick and stiff. Add colouring and flavouring if liked. Quickly pour into a greased 28 × 18-cm (11 × 7-in) Swiss roll tin and dust the top with your chosen coating. Leave for 24 hours. Remove from the tin and cut into squares (scissors are best to use). Roll each cut side again in your chosen coating. Serve with Raspberry sauce (opposite) if liked. Store in an airtight tin. (They will keep for 2–3 weeks.) **Makes 350 g/12 oz.**

Use a mixture of caster sugar and ground cinnamon to sprinkle over hot buttered toast, to dredge over hot doughnuts or to sprinkle over plain biscuit dough. To make pinwheel cookies, roll out a thin sheet of biscuit dough and sprinkle generously with cinnamon sugar, then roll up tightly and cut into thin slices.

Toasted Marshmallows with Raspberry Sauce

(Illustrated on page 71)

These are an ideal treat that children can cook for themselves on a barbecue or bonfire. Give them a long skewer and thread on the marshmallows. Twirl the marshmallows around in front of the coals until completely toasted. They can then be dipped into melted chocolate or into a raspberry sauce before eating.

Raspberry Sauce

METRIC		IMPERIAL
225 g	fresh or frozen raspberries	8 oz
150 ml	water	$\frac{1}{4}$ pint
	caster sugar to taste	
1 teaspoon	cornflour	1 teaspoon

Place the raspberries and water in a saucepan and bring to the boil. Sieve or blend in a liquidiser or food processor and return to the pan. Add caster sugar to taste. Mix the cornflour with a little raspberry juice. Stir into the purée. Bring to the boil, stirring all the time until thickened. **Makes 300 ml/$\frac{1}{2}$ pint.**

Note: This sauce is delicious served with ice cream or fresh fruit.

SWEETS

Country Apple Pie

METRIC		IMPERIAL
225 g	shortcrust pastry	8 oz
	(see Treacle tart, page 68)	
450 g	quinces	1 lb
450 g	cooking apples	1 lb
25–50 g	soft light golden sugar	1–2 oz
1 teaspoon	ground cinnamon	1 teaspoon
2 tablespoons	water	2 tablespoons
	a little egg white	
1 tablespoon	caster sugar	1 tablespoon
	cream, to serve	

Roll out the pastry 5 cm (2 in) wider than a 1.15-litre (2-pint) pie dish. Cut off a 2.5-cm (1-in) ring from the pastry and place it around the rim of the buttered dish.

Peel, core and slice the quinces and apples, and layer the fruit alternately with the sugar and cinnamon. Add water. Cover dish with pastry, damp edges and seal firmly. Trim and flute. Make a hole in the centre. Brush the top with egg white and sprinkle with caster sugar then place in a moderately hot oven (200 c/400 f/gas 6) and bake for 20 minutes. Lower the oven to moderate (180 c/350 f/gas 4) and cook for a further 30 minutes. Serve hot with cream. **Serves 4–6.**

Crème Caramel

METRIC		IMPERIAL
75 g	granulated sugar	3 oz
4 tablespoons	water	4 tablespoons
50 g	caster sugar	2 oz
600 ml	milk, warm	1 pint
$\frac{1}{2}$ teaspoon	vanilla essence	$\frac{1}{2}$ teaspoon
3	eggs, size 3	3
1	egg yolk, size 3	1

Dissolve the granulated sugar in the water and boil until golden brown. Remove from heat. Pour the warm caramel into eight small ramekin dishes, coating the sides and base. Dissolve the caster sugar in the warm milk with the vanilla essence. Beat in the eggs and additional yolk. Strain into the prepared dishes. Place in a roasting tin half-filled with water in a moderate oven (180 c/350 f/gas 4) and cook for 30–45 minutes or until set. Chill in the refrigerator overnight before serving. **Serves 8.**

When making a cake, caster sugar gives the creamed mixture greater volume and yields a lighter sponge because it dissolves readily.

Carrot Cake

(Illustrated opposite)

METRIC		IMPERIAL
50 g	carrots, finely grated	2 oz
75 g	self-raising flour, sifted	3 oz
50 g	chopped walnuts	2 oz
3	eggs, size 1	3
100 g	caster sugar	4 oz
3 tablespoons	apricot jam	3 tablespoons
50 ml	whipped cream	$\frac{1}{2}$ pint

Put the carrot, flour and nuts into a mixing bowl. Whisk the eggs and sugar together over a saucepan of hot water until the mixture is thick and creamy and leaves a trail when the whisk is lifted up. With a spatula or metal spoon carefully fold in the carrot mixture. Divide the mixture evenly into two lined 18-cm (7-in) sandwich tins. Place in a moderately hot oven (190 c/ 375 f/gas 5) and bake for 15–20 minutes. Cool on a cooling tray. When cold, sandwich together with the jam and whipped cream. **Serves 8–10.**

Carrot Cake and Apple and Pear Round (page 77)

74

Chocolate Nut Bars

METRIC		IMPERIAL
75 g	butter or margarine	3 oz
100 g	plain flour, sifted	4 oz
75 g	porridge oats	3 oz
$\frac{1}{2}$ teaspoon	baking powder	$\frac{1}{2}$ teaspoon
100 g	soft light golden sugar	4 oz
	Topping	
175 g	plain chocolate	6 oz
50 g	butter or margarine	2 oz
175 g	golden syrup	6 oz
100 g	chopped walnuts	4 oz

Melt the butter in a saucepan and stir in the flour, oats, baking powder and sugar. Press into the base of a 23 × 33-cm (9 × 13-in) Swiss roll tin. Place in a moderate oven (180 c/350 f/gas 4) and cook for 10 minutes.

Make the topping. Melt the chocolate with the butter and syrup. Stir in the nuts, spread over the cooked base and cool in the tin. Cut into 24 bars. Store in an airtight tin. (They will keep for 1–2 weeks.) **Makes 24.**

Plum Duff

METRIC		IMPERIAL
400 g	frozen puff pastry, thawed	14 oz
2–3 tablespoons	milk	2–3 tablespoons
1 tablespoon	granulated sugar	1 tablespoon
675 g	fresh plums, stoned and washed	$1\frac{1}{2}$ lb
300 ml	single cream	$\frac{1}{2}$ pint
25 g	caster sugar	1 oz
3	eggs, size 3, beaten	3
	cream, to serve	

Line a 1.15-litre (2-pint) oval ovenproof dish with pastry and decorate the edges with left-over twists of pastry. Prick the base and line with greaseproof paper and baking beans. Glaze the pastry with a little milk and granulated sugar. Place in a hot oven

(220 c/425 f/gas 7) and bake for 20 minutes. Remove paper and beans and cook for a further 10 minutes in a moderately hot oven (190 c/375 f/gas 5) until the base is cooked. Leave to cool, then fill with the plums. Mix together the cream and sugar over a gentle heat, add the eggs and strain. Pour over the plums and bake for a further 40 minutes in a moderately hot oven (190 c/375 f/gas 5) until just set. Serve hot or cold with fresh cream.
Serves 4.

Apple and Pear Round

(Illustrated on page 75)

METRIC		IMPERIAL
225 g	**plain flour, sifted**	8 oz
$\frac{1}{2}$ teaspoon	**salt**	$\frac{1}{2}$ teaspoon
2 teaspoons	**baking powder**	2 teaspoons
50 g	**butter**	2 oz
1	**medium cooking apple**	1
1	**dessert pear**	1
50 g	**caster sugar**	2 oz
4 tablespoons	**milk**	4 tablespoons
	Glaze	
	a little milk	
1 tablespoon	**demerara sugar**	1 tablespoon

Mix together the flour, salt and baking powder. Rub in the butter. Peel, core and coarsely grate the apple and pear. Add the sugar, grated fruit and sufficient milk to give a soft but not sticky dough, turn the mixture on to a floured surface and knead lightly. Roll out to a 20-cm (8-in) circle and place on a greased and floured baking sheet. Score the round into eight pieces. Brush the top with milk and sprinkle with sugar. Place in a moderately hot oven (200 c/400 f/gas 6) and bake for 20–25 minutes or until golden brown. Serve warm with butter.
Serves 8.

Cook's Tips

For a professional finish to a simple cake, dredge the top heavily with icing sugar and mark lines on it using a very hot metal skewer. The lines can be parallel or criss-cross. Puff pastry also looks good finished in this way.

Apple and Date Chutney

(Illustrated opposite)

METRIC		IMPERIAL
450 g	cooking apples	1 lb
450 g	dates	1 lb
100 g	preserved stem ginger	4 oz
225 g	sultanas	8 oz
225 g	soft rich dark sugar	8 oz
40 g	salt	$1\frac{1}{2}$ oz
600 ml	malt vinegar	1 pint

Peel, core and slice the cooking apples. Stone the dates. Chop the ginger. Place all the ingredients in a preserving pan. Bring to the boil and cook until mixture thickens. Pour the chutney into warm sterilised jars, seal and label. **Makes 1.75 kg (4 lb).**

Plum Jam

(Illustrated opposite)

METRIC		IMPERIAL
2.75 kg	plums	6 lb
1 litre	water	$1\frac{3}{4}$ pints
2.75 kg	preserving sugar	6 lb

Stone the plums, reserving some of the stones, rinse in cold water and drain, then put the fruit into a preserving pan. Crack the reserved stones and remove the kernels. Add the kernels and water to the fruit, and simmer for about 30 minutes or until the fruit is soft. Add the warmed sugar, stirring until dissolved. Clip a sugar thermometer to the pan and boil rapidly to 104 c/ 220 f is reached. (If not using a thermometer, place a little of the jam on a cold saucer. The surface should pucker when touched.) Pour jam into warm sterilised jam jars, seal and label. **Makes 4.5 kg (10 lb).**

Clockwise from top left: Apple and Date Chutney, Lemon Curd (page 81), Mincemeat (page 82) and Plum Jam

Damson Syrup

METRIC		IMPERIAL
450 g	damsons	1 lb
150 ml	water	$\frac{1}{4}$ pint
350 g	preserving sugar for each	12 oz
	600 ml (1 pint) of juice	

Put the fruit and water into the top of a double saucepan or in a basin standing in a pan of simmering water. Press down the fruit well and cook for about 1 hour until all the juice is extracted. Continue to press down frequently during cooking. Strain through a jelly bag or through several layers of muslin over a fine sieve. Measure the juice and add the appropriate quantity of sugar. Heat together until the sugar has dissolved, stirring well. Pour the syrup into hot bottling jars with well-fitting screw tops, leaving a 2-cm ($\frac{3}{4}$-in) space to allow for expansion. Stand bottles and jars in a deep pan with a rack at the bottom. Loosen screw band half a turn and put sufficient water into the pan. To cover the liquid level in the jars the water should be heated to simmering, *not* boiling, point and the temperature maintained for 30 minutes. The jars should be removed with heatproof gloves and the screw tops tightened immediately and allowed to cool. (The syrup will keep for 6 months in a cool dark place.) **Makes 600–900 ml (1–1$\frac{1}{2}$ pints).**

Variations
Use the method for damson syrup, with the following variations:

Blackcurrant Syrup: Use 450 g (1 lb) blackcurrants instead of the damsons.

Raspberry Syrup: Use 450 g (1 lb) raspberries instead of the damsons and the same quantity of sugar as for damson syrup (no water is required for this variation).

Blackberry and Apple Cheese

METRIC		IMPERIAL
450 g	cooking apples	1 lb
1 kg	blackberries, thawed if frozen	2 lb
1	lemon, juice only	1
300 ml	water	$\frac{1}{2}$ pint
450 g	granulated sugar for each	1 lb
	450 g (1 lb) of fruit pulp	

Peel, core and chop the apples. Place the blackberries, apples, lemon juice and water in a saucepan. Simmer gently until soft. Sieve or blend in a liquidiser or food processor. Measure the pulp, return to the pan, add the appropriate amount of sugar and allow to dissolve. Cook gently, stirring, until the mixture is very thick and leaves a definite impression when the spoon is removed. Cool a little then pour into a 1-kg (2-lb) greased loaf tin. Chill well. Turn out on to a serving plate. Serve with scones or bread. If liked, bottle in warm sterilised jars (this keeps well up to 1 year). But, once opened, store covered in a refrigerator. Eat as soon as possible. **Makes 800 g (1$\frac{3}{4}$ lb).**

Lemon Curd

(Illustrated on page 79)

METRIC		IMPERIAL
575 g	caster or granulated sugar	1$\frac{1}{4}$ lb
5	lemons, finely grated rind and juice	5
150 g	unsalted butter	5 oz
5	eggs, size 3, well beaten	5

Put all the ingredients into the top of a double saucepan or in a basin standing in a pan of simmering water. Stir until the sugar has dissolved, stirring from time to time until the curd thickens. Pour into warm sterilised jars. Seal, label and store in a cool place. Use within 2 months. **Makes 1.5 kg (3 lb).**

Variations
Orange Curd: Replace the lemons with 3 large oranges and $\frac{1}{2}$ lemon. Use only 400 g (14 oz) sugar.

Mincemeat

(Illustrated on page 79)

METRIC		IMPERIAL
50 g	blanched almonds, chopped	2 oz
225 g	apples, peeled, cored and grated	8 oz
350 g	raisins, chopped	12 oz
350 g	sultanas, chopped	12 oz
225 g	currants, chopped	8 oz
100 g	mixed peel, chopped	4 oz
225 g	suet, chopped	8 oz
350 g	demerara sugar	12 oz
150 ml	brandy or rum	$\frac{1}{4}$ pint
1	lemon, grated rind and juice	1

Mix all the ingredients together in a large mixing bowl, cover with cling film and leave for 48 hours, stirring occasionally. Bottle in clean sterilised jars. Label and store in a dark place. Use within 3 months. **Makes 2–2$\frac{1}{2}$ kg (4–5 lb).**

DRINKS

Cider Sparkle

(Illustrated opposite)

METRIC		IMPERIAL
1 litre	dry cider	1$\frac{3}{4}$ pints
150 ml	gin	$\frac{1}{4}$ pint
2 tablespoons	golden syrup	2 tablespoons
1	lemon, juice and rind	1
	(rind cut into strips)	
2	green dessert apples,	2
	cored and quartered	
	ice cubes	

Chill the cider and gin. Pour into a punch bowl. Blend in the syrup, lemon juice and rind, apples and ice cubes. **Serves 12.**

Clockwise from the top: Cider Sparkle, Mulled Wine (page 85) and Sherry Posset (page 84)

Bramley Punch

METRIC		IMPERIAL
450 g	Bramley apples	1 lb
750 ml	water	1¼ pints
3 tablespoons	golden syrup	3 tablespoons
1 teaspoon	ground cinnamon	1 teaspoon
1	bottle sparkling wine	1
	ice cubes	

Soak a whole or halved sugar cube in angostura bitters and use it in a pink gin or in champagne cocktails.

Peel, core and roughly chop the apples. Put them into a saucepan with the water and cook until soft. Pour the mixture into a liquidiser or food processor, together with the golden syrup and cinnamon. Blend until a fine purée is formed. Allow to cool. Pour into a punch bowl and stir in the bottle of sparkling wine and ice cubes immediately before serving. **Serves 10.**

Sherry Posset

(Illustrated on page 83)

METRIC		IMPERIAL
600 ml	milk	1 pint
300 ml	medium sherry	½ pint
300 ml	brown ale	½ pint
1 tablespoon	soft rich dark sugar	1 tablespoon
1 teaspoon	ground nutmeg	1 teaspoon

Warm the milk in a saucepan. In another saucepan heat the sherry, brown ale and sugar until they boil. Slowly pour the mixture into the milk, stirring continuously. Pour into mugs and serve sprinkled with nutmeg. **Serves 6.**

Mulled Wine

(Illustrated on page 83)

METRIC		IMPERIAL
1	bottle red wine	1
1 tablespoon	granulated sugar	1 tablespoon
1 teaspoon	ground nutmeg	1 teaspoon
4	egg yolks, size 3	4

Pour the red wine into a saucepan with the sugar and nutmeg. Heat gently until the sugar has dissolved, whisk in the egg yolks stirring all the time. Heat until the mixture thickens. Spoon it into mugs and serve immediately. **Serves 8.**

Warming Punch

METRIC		IMPERIAL
2	oranges, quartered and studded with cloves	2
150 ml	brandy	$\frac{1}{4}$ pint
2 tablespoons	soft rich dark sugar	2 tablespoons
2	cinnamon sticks	2
2	bottles rosé wine	2
150 ml	red vermouth	$\frac{1}{4}$ pint

Put the oranges, brandy, sugar and cinnamon sticks in a saucepan and heat very gently until warm. Pour in the wine and vermouth and heat slowly until just warm. Transfer to a punch bowl and ladle into glasses to serve. **Serves 12.**

Cook's Tips

A spoonful of sugar or a sugar cube added to the water in a vase of flowers will help the blooms to stay fresh longer.

Winter

Amidst the cold days of
winter we celebrate the
warmest and richest feast of
the old year – Christmas
– then we rejoice in the
nostalgia of the New Year's
Eve gatherings.

Winter Menu

— * —

Herbed Pears

— * —

Glazed Stuffed Gammon

— * —

Cold Christmas Pudding

Herbed Pears

(Illustrated on pages 86/87)

METRIC		IMPERIAL
6	firm dessert pears	6
300 ml	double cream	½ pint
2 tablespoons	herb vinegar	2 tablespoons
50 g	caster sugar	2 oz
	salt and freshly ground	
	black pepper	
	Garnish	
	parsley or fresh tarragon	

Peel and halve each pear. Scoop out and discard the core. Beat the cream, vinegar, caster sugar and seasoning together. Place two halves of the pears, rounded side up, on individual serving plates. Spoon the cream over the top and garnish with fresh herbs. **Serves 6.**

Variation
Use raspberry or another fruit vinegar of your choice.

Glazed Stuffed Gammon

(Illustrated on pages 86/87)

METRIC		IMPERIAL
2.25–2.75 kg	gammon, boned and soaked overnight	5–6 lb
	Stuffing	
75 g	ground almonds	3 oz
100 g	white or brown breadcrumbs	4 oz
100 g	dried apricots, chopped	4 oz
1 tablespoon	chopped parsley	1 tablespoon
1	onion, chopped	1
25 g	demerara sugar	1 oz
50 g	butter, melted	2 oz
1	egg, size 3	1
	Glaze	
50 g	demerara or soft light golden sugar or	2 oz
3–4 tablespoons	golden syrup	3–4 tablespoons

Mix the stuffing. Stir all the ingredients until the mixture binds together. If the mixture is a little stiff add a little hot water until the required consistency is reached.

Place the stuffing in the boned gammon cavity. Using a roasting tin with a trivet, stand the gammon on the trivet with the tin filled with about 5 mm ($\frac{1}{2}$ inch) cold water. Cover with kitchen foil, place in a moderately hot oven (200 c/400 F/gas 6) and bake for $1\frac{1}{2}$ hours. Leave to cool a little, then remove the skin carefully.

Score the fat to make a pretty diamond pattern. Rub in the sugar or brush on the golden syrup. Put the joint in a dry roasting tin, place in a hot oven (220 c/425 F/gas 7) and bake for about 25–30 minutes. Serve with mashed potato, and puréed carrots and swedes. **Serves 10–12.**

Variations
If preferred, stud each diamond of fat with a whole clove, or use drained pineapple rings placed on top of the sugar and secured in position with cocktail sticks.

Give flavour to boiled salted beef or boiled gammon by adding a tablespoon of treacle and a whole orange to the cooking liquid.

Cold Christmas Pudding

(Illustrated on pages 86/87)

METRIC		IMPERIAL
450 ml	whipping or double cream	$\frac{3}{4}$ pint
2	eggs, size 1, separated	2
1 tablespoon	coffee essence	1 tablespoon
90 g	icing sugar, sifted	$3\frac{1}{2}$ oz
1 teaspoon	ground mixed spice	1 teaspoon
100 g	brown or white breadcrumbs	4 oz
100 g	raisins	4 oz
50 g	sultanas	2 oz
4 tablespoons	brandy	4 tablespoons
50 g	chopped nuts	2 oz
50 g	chopped mixed peel	2 oz
50 g	dates, stoned and chopped	2 oz
100 g	glacé cherries, halved	4 oz
	Decoration	
150 ml	double cream, whipped	$\frac{1}{4}$ pint
	sprig of holly	

At Christmas time dip a cube of sugar in warm brandy, then ignite it on top of the pudding.

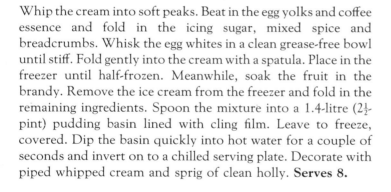

Whip the cream into soft peaks. Beat in the egg yolks and coffee essence and fold in the icing sugar, mixed spice and breadcrumbs. Whisk the egg whites in a clean grease-free bowl until stiff. Fold gently into the cream with a spatula. Place in the freezer until half-frozen. Meanwhile, soak the fruit in the brandy. Remove the ice cream from the freezer and fold in the remaining ingredients. Spoon the mixture into a 1.4-litre ($2\frac{1}{2}$-pint) pudding basin lined with cling film. Leave to freeze, covered. Dip the basin quickly into hot water for a couple of seconds and invert on to a chilled serving plate. Decorate with piped whipped cream and sprig of clean holly. **Serves 8.**

Dundee Cake (page 93), Cherry Shortbread and Almond Crunch (both on page 97)

Fudge

METRIC		IMPERIAL
50 g	**butter**	2 oz
2 tablespoons	**golden syrup**	2 tablespoons
450 g	**granulated sugar**	1 lb
8 tablespoons	**condensed milk**	8 tablespoons
½ teaspoon	**vanilla essence**	½ teaspoon
4 tablespoons	**water**	4 tablespoons

Place all the ingredients in a heavy-based pan. Heat slowly until the sugar has dissolved. Bring to the boil, stirring continuously. Clip a sugar thermometer to the pan and cook to 114 c/238 F stirring all the time to prevent the mixture sticking. (If not using a thermometer, drop a little of the mixture in cold water. It should form a soft ball when gathered up with finger and thumb.) Remove from the heat. Whisk until the mixture thickens and goes pale in colour (it is best to use an electric whisk). Pour into a buttered 18-cm (7-in) square tin. Cut into 2.5-cm (1-in) squares when cool. Store in a cardboard container to prevent hardening. **Makes about 50 pieces.**

Cranberry Oat Bars

METRIC		IMPERIAL
175 g	**rolled oats**	6 oz
100 g	**soft light golden sugar**	4 oz
75 g	**butter**	3 oz
50 g	**golden syrup**	2 oz
50 g	**cranberries, thawed if frozen**	2 oz

Mix the oats and sugar together in a mixing bowl. Melt the butter and syrup together and stir into the dry ingredients then stir in the cranberries. Press into a greased square 20-cm (8-in) tin, place in a moderately hot oven (190 c/375 F/gas 5) and bake for 20–25 minutes. Allow to cool slightly then mark into fingers. Leave to go cold then remove from tin. Store in an airtight tin. (They will keep for 4–5 days.) **Makes 12 bars.**

Dundee Cake

(Illustrated on page 91)

METRIC		IMPERIAL
225 g	butter or margarine	8 oz
225 g	caster sugar	8 oz
4	eggs, size 3	4
225 g	plain flour, sifted	8 oz
350 g	sultanas	12 oz
275 g	currants	10 oz
200 g	chopped mixed peel	7 oz
100 g	glacé cherries	4 oz
1	small orange, finely grated rind only	1
	Decoration	
50–75 g	blanched whole almonds	2–3 oz

Cream the butter and sugar together until light and fluffy. Beat the eggs into the mixture a little at a time, taking care not to curdle the mixture. Fold in the flour, fruit and rind. Spoon the mixture into a lined 20-cm (8-in) round deep-sided cake tin. Smooth the top and arrange the whole almonds in a pretty pattern on top of the cake. Place in a cool oven (150 c/300 f/gas 2) and bake for about 3½ hours or until a skewer inserted in the cake comes out clean. (If the cake is cooking too quickly cover the top with a damp sheet of greaseproof paper to prevent overcooking.) Leave to cool in the tin for 45 minutes before turning out. **Makes 16–18 slices.**

Note: This cake is ideal if wrapped in foil or greaseproof paper and kept in an airtight tin for 1 month before eating.

Cook's Tips

Use all granulated sugar or half and half granulated and icing sugar to give home-made marzipan an interesting texture. Granulated sugar can also be used to give brandy butter more texture.

Coconut Ice

(Illustrated opposite)

METRIC		IMPERIAL
200 ml	condensed milk	7 fl oz
475 g	icing sugar, sifted	17 oz
250 g	desiccated coconut	9 oz
	red food colouring	

Mix together milk and icing sugar. Knead in the coconut. Divide the mixture into two halves. Cover one half and knead the other well, pressing into a square buttered 15–18-cm (6–7-in) tin. Add a little red food colouring to the remaining half and knead until the colour is evenly mixed. Press this mixture into the tin. Leave to set. Cut into 2.5-cm (1-in) squares. Store in an airtight tin. (It will keep for about 1 week.) **Serves 6.**

Use icing sugar to make extra smooth textured shortbread dough.

Butterscotch

(Illustrated opposite)

METRIC		IMPERIAL
225 g	caster sugar	8 oz
225 g	demerara or granulated sugar	8 oz
150 ml	water and milk, mixed	$\frac{1}{4}$ pint
225 g	golden syrup	8 oz
50 g	butter	2 oz

Place all the ingredients in a large saucepan. Clip a sugar thermometer to the pan and heat, stirring occasionally, to 145 c/280 f. (If not using a thermometer, the mixture should thicken and form a brittle thread when the spoon is lifted from the mixture.) Pour into a 28 × 18-cm (11 × 7-in) Swiss roll tin lined with silicone paper and mark into squares when cool. Store in an airtight tin. (It will keep for about 1 week.) **Makes 60–70 pieces.**

Note: For a really creamy butterscotch replace the water and milk with cream.

Marzipan Fruits (page 96), Coconut Ice and Butterscotch

Marzipan Fruits

(Illustrated on page 95)

METRIC		IMPERIAL
225 g	icing sugar, sifted	8 oz
225 g	caster sugar	8 oz
450 g	ground almonds	1 lb
2	eggs, size 3, beaten	2
1 teaspoon	vanilla essence	1 teaspoon
	lemon juice to taste	
	To finish	
	food colouring,	
	caster sugar, coffee essence etc.	
	(see below)	

Mix sugars and almonds together. Add beaten eggs, vanilla essence and lemon juice. Knead until stiff and pliable. Keep covered until required. Use varied food colourings and caster sugar as necessary to make the fruits of your choice.

Apples: Colour the marzipan green, form into apple shapes and, using a fine paint brush and pink food colouring, shade one side to look like a ripening apple. Press a clove into the base and use angelica for a stalk.

Bananas: Colour marzipan yellow, form into banana shapes, and, using a fine paint brush and strong black coffee, brush the brown stripes of a banana.

Pears: As for apples but form into pear shapes.

Strawberries: Colour marzipan with red colouring, form into strawberry shapes, top with leaf shapes made from green marzipan. Make indentations in the strawberry with a cocktail stick and tip into caster sugar.

Acorns: Colour marzipan pale brown with coffee essence and form into acorn shapes. Dip the lower half into a little egg white then chocolate vermicelli to form the cup.

Oranges: Colour the marzipan orange. Form into small rounds. Roll over a fine grater to make the finish. Put a clove in the centre top of each orange.

Glaze plain biscuits or
shortcrust pastry pie
crusts with icing sugar
mixed with a little water,
then return to the oven
until pale coffee coloured.

Cherry Shortbread

(Illustrated on page 91)

METRIC		IMPERIAL
150 g	plain flour, sifted	5 oz
25 g	rice flour	1 oz
	pinch of salt	
50 g	caster suger	2 oz
100 g	butter	4 oz
25 g	glacé cherries, chopped	1 oz

Put the dry ingredients into a mixing bowl, knead in the butter
and, when a soft dough is formed, add the cherries. Knead until
free of cracks. Press into an 18-cm (7-in) sandwich tin base-lined
with greaseproof paper. Smooth down, crimp edges with a fork
and mark into six pieces. Place in a cool oven (150 c/300 f/gas 2)
and bake for 50–60 minutes. Dredge with caster sugar when
cooked and cut into wedges when cold. Store, wrapped in cling
film, in an airtight tin. (It will keep for 1–2 weeks.) **Serves 6–8.**

Variation

Wholemeal Shortbread: Replace the plain flour with
wholemeal flour and omit the cherries.

Almond Crunch

(Illustrated on page 91)

METRIC		IMPERIAL
225 g	blanched almonds, toasted	8 oz
225 g	caster sugar	8 oz
225 g	butter	8 oz
1 tablespoon	lemon juice	1 tablespoon

Roughly chop the almonds. Put the sugar and butter in a heavy-
based saucepan and stir until all the sugar melts. Add the nuts.
Clip a sugar thermometer to the pan and cook over a moderate
heat to 150 c/300 f. (If not using a thermometer, check the
colour of the syrup – it should turn dark brown.) Take off the
heat and stir in the lemon juice. Pour immediately into a lined
20-cm (8-in) square tin. When completely cold break into pieces
– store in an airtight container. (It will keep for about 1 week.)
Serves 6–8.

Chocolate Pots

METRIC		IMPERIAL
4	eggs, size 3	4
100 g	caster sugar	4 oz
600 ml	hot milk	1 pint
175 g	plain chocolate, melted	6 oz
1 teaspoon	finely grated orange rind	1 teaspoon

Whisk the eggs in a basin over simmering water. Add the sugar slowly, whisking all the time, until the mixture is pale, falls in a thick ribbon and the whisk leaves a trail when lifted. Add the hot milk in a steady stream, whisking constantly. Add the chocolate and orange rind. Pour into four greased ramekin dishes. Place in a roasting tin and pour in 2.5 cm (1 in) of hot water. Bake in a moderate oven (160 c/325 f/gas 3) for 40–50 minutes. Chill overnight before serving. **Serves 4.**

Fruity Clafoutis

(Illustrated opposite)

METRIC		IMPERIAL
3	eggs, size 3	3
3 tablespoons	plain flour, sifted	3 tablespoons
	pinch of salt	
5 tablespoons	caster sugar	5 tablespoons
450 ml	milk	$\frac{3}{4}$ pint
675 g	cherries	$1\frac{1}{2}$ lb
25 g	unsalted butter	1 oz

Beat the eggs lightly, blend in the flour, salt and half the sugar. Warm the milk and gradually pour into the egg mixture, stirring continuously. Put the cherries into a buttered 20-cm (8-in) oval shallow ovenproof dish, pour the batter over them, and dot with the butter. Bake in a hot oven (220 c/425 f/gas 7) for 25–30 minutes or until set, with the cherries near the surface. Serve sprinkled with the remaining sugar. **Serves 6.**

From the top: Fruity Clafoutis and Chestnut Meringue (page 101)

Snowy Yule Log

(Illustrated on page 103)

METRIC		IMPERIAL
50 g	caster sugar	2 oz
2	eggs, size 1	2
1 tablespoon	cocoa powder, sifted	1 tablespoon
50 g	plain flour, sifted	2 oz
2 tablespoons	warm water	2 tablespoons
	a little extra caster sugar	
	Filling and topping	
100 g	butter	4 oz
225 g	icing sugar, sifted	8 oz
100 g	plain chocolate, melted	4 oz
1 teaspoon	coffee essence	1 teaspoon
	Decorations	
1	small Shreddie	1
50 g	ready-made marzipan	2 oz
	green food colouring	
2	robins	2
	a little icing sugar, sifted	2

Whisk the caster sugar and eggs in a large mixing bowl over a saucepan of hot water until the mixture is thick and creamy and trebled in volume. It should look pale and be thick enough to leave a trail when the whisk is lifted up. Remove from the heat and fold in the cocoa, plain flour and water. Pour the mixture into a greased and lined 13 × 23-cm (6 × 9-in) Swiss roll tin. Place in a moderately hot oven (200 c/400 f/gas 6) and bake for 12–14 minutes or until well risen and firm to the touch. Sprinkle caster sugar on a piece of oblong greaseproof paper that is slightly larger than the Swiss roll. When cooked, turn the sponge on to the sugared paper. Carefully remove the lining paper and trim 6 mm ($\frac{1}{4}$ in) off the crusty sides. Using the back of a fork make a small indentation along one short edge of sponge to make it easier to roll. Cover the sponge with a sheet of greaseproof paper and roll up loosely.

Make the filling. Cream the butter and sifted icing sugar together. Add the chocolate and the coffee essence. Unroll the sponge and spread half the filling over the surface then re-roll into a log. Use the remaining filling to cover the surface of the log. Fork lines on the log to represent the bark. Mix the marzipan with a few drops of green colouring. Roll and shape the green marzipan into ivy leaves on a stem and wrap around the log. Decorate with robins and the Shreddie made into a nest, and dust with icing sugar. **Serves 8–12.**

Chestnut Meringue

(Illustrated on page 99)

METRIC		IMPERIAL
4	egg whites, size 2	4
	pinch of salt	
225 g	icing sugar, sifted	8 oz
	Filling and topping	
75 g	tube of crème de marrons	$2\frac{3}{4}$ oz
	(sweetened chestnut purée)	
300 ml	double cream, whipped	$\frac{1}{2}$ pint
25 g	plain chocolate, grated	1 oz
2 tablespoons	icing sugar, sifted	2 tablespoons

Using a hand-held or electric whisk, whisk the egg whites and salt in a clean grease-free bowl until soft peaks form. Gradually add all the icing sugar. Keep whisking until the meringue forms firm peaks and becomes smooth and glossy. Divide the mixture between two baking sheets lined with silicone paper and spread carefully into two 20-cm (8-in) rounds. Place in a cool oven (140 c/275 f/gas 1) and bake for 1–1½ hours until crisp. Leave to cool, then peel off the silicone paper.

Meanwhile, prepare the filling and topping. Gently fold the crème de marrons into half the cream and place the remaining cream into a nylon piping bag with a star vegetable nozzle. Place one meringue round on to a serving plate and pile on the crème de marrons filling. Place the other meringue round on top. Decorate with rosettes of cream and grated chocolate. Dust with icing sugar. **Serves 6 8.**

Cook's Tips

A cube of sugar is just the answer if you have run out of birthday cake candles. Drain a small can of apricot halves and arrange the pieces of fruit round the edge of the cake, placing the cut side uppermost. Soak some sugar lumps in lemon essence, put one in each apricot half and light with a match.

Stollen

(Illustrated opposite)

METRIC		IMPERIAL
225 g	**strong plain flour, sifted and warmed**	8 oz
	pinch of salt	
15 g	**dried yeast**	$\frac{1}{2}$ oz
5 tablespoons	**warmed milk**	5 tablespoons
50 g	**caster sugar**	2 oz
50 g	**butter, melted**	2 oz
1	**egg, size 3, beaten**	1
100 g	**ground almonds**	4 oz
25 g	**flaked almonds**	1 oz
25 g	**glacé cherries, chopped**	1 oz
20 g	**chopped mixed peel**	$\frac{3}{4}$ oz
75 g	**mixed dried fruit**	3 oz
25 g	**butter, softened**	1 oz
	Topping	
25 g	**icing sugar, sifted**	1 oz
$\frac{1}{2}$ teaspoon	**ground cinnamon**	$\frac{1}{2}$ teaspoon

A cube of sugar put into a vacuum flask will keep it fresh if it is to be stored away for some time.

Put the flour and salt into a warmed mixing bowl. In a separate bowl, sprinkle the yeast on to the milk with a pinch of the caster sugar. Leave to one side until very frothy and doubled in size. Add the yeast mixture to the flour with the melted butter, sugar and egg. Mix until smooth with a wooden spoon. When the dough comes away cleanly when beaten against the side of the bowl turn the mixture on to a floured surface. Knead for 5 minutes. Cover and leave the dough in a warm place for 45–50 minutes or until doubled in size. Knead lightly, then knead in the almonds, cherries, peel and dried fruit. Cover and leave again for a further 40 minutes in a warm place until risen. Turn on to a floured surface and roll out to an oval of about 20 × 25 cm (8 × 10 in). Spread on the softened butter. Fold together lengthways and shape into a crescent. Press the damped dough edges together. Place the stollen on a greased baking tray and leave for 30 minutes to rise. Place in a moderately hot oven at (200 c/400 f/gas 6) and bake for 30–35 minutes. When cooked and warm dredge the stollen with the icing sugar and cinnamon sieved together. Store in an airtight tin. (It will keep for 1–2 weeks.) **Serves 8–10.**

Snowy Yule Log (page 100) and Stollen

Baked Cheesecake

METRIC		IMPERIAL
350 g	sweet flan pastry	12 oz
	(see Soft fruit pie, page 48)	
	Filling	
50 g	butter	2 oz
25 g	caster sugar	1 oz
275 g	curd cheese	10 oz
25 g	sultanas	1 oz
1	egg, size 3, beaten	1
1	lemon, grated rind only	1
25 g	chopped mixed peel	1 oz
	few drops of vanilla essence	

Roll out the pastry and use to line a greased 23-cm (9-in) flan ring. Mix the butter and sugar together. Add all the other ingredients and mix thoroughly. Pour into flan ring and make a lattice-work with any remaining pastry. Place in a moderate oven (180 c/350 f/gas 4) and bake for 40–50 minutes or until set. **Serves 6.**

Chocolate Cream

METRIC		IMPERIAL
2	dessert pears	2
2	eggs, size 3, separated	2
40 g	caster sugar	1½ oz
100 g	milk chocolate	4 oz
300 ml	natural yogurt	½ pint
15 g	powdered gelatine	½ oz
3 tablespoons	hot water	3 tablespoons
150 ml	whipped cream	¼ pint
	Decoration	
	crystallised violets (see page 61)	

Peel, core and purée the pears. Cream the egg yolks and sugar until fluffy. Melt the chocolate in warmed yogurt in a bowl over a saucepan of hot water. Whisk in the egg yolks and heat gently until the mixture coats the back of the spoon. Sprinkle the gelatine on to the hot water and leave to dissolve. Whisk the dissolved gelatine into the egg yolk mixture. Whisk the egg whites. Fold in the purée, egg whites and half of the cream. Pour into a 900-ml (1½-pint) jelly mould rinsed in cold water and leave to set in the refrigerator. Turn out and decorate with the remaining cream and crystallised violets. **Serves 6.**

Sprinkle granulated sugar over a not-too-rich fruit cake before baking and it will come out of the oven with a lovely light crust.

Rhubarb and Fig Jam

(Illustrated on page 107)

METRIC		IMPERIAL
1 kg	rhubarb, roughly chopped	2 lb
450 g	dried figs, chopped	1 lb
3 tablespoons	lemon juice	3 tablespoons
4 tablespoons	water	4 tablespoons
1.5 kg	preserving sugar, warmed	3 lb

Put the rhubarb, figs, lemon juice and water into a saucepan and heat gently until the juices start to run, then cook until fruits are soft. Add the warmed sugar, clip a sugar thermometer to the pan and cook to 104 c/220 f. (If not using a thermometer, place a little of the jam on a cold saucer. The surface should pucker slightly when touched.) Pour into warm sterilised 450-g (1-lb) jars, cover, seal and label immediately. (It will keep for about 1 year.) **Makes 2–3 jars.**

Clementines in Brandy

(Illustrated on page 107)

METRIC		IMPERIAL
1¾ kg	clementines	4 lb
450 g	preserving sugar	1 lb
600 ml	water	1 pint
475 ml	brandy	16 fl oz

Peel the clementines and leave them whole. Dissolve the sugar in the water, bring to the boil then allow to cool. Add the brandy. Pack the fruit tightly into 450-g (1-lb) sterilised bottling jars and cover with the cold syrup. Seal. (They will keep for about 1 month). **Makes 6 jars.**

Variations

If preferred use peaches, nectarines, cherries or pineapple instead of clementines. For a spicy version add 1–2 small cinnamon sticks and 25 g (1 oz) whole blanched almonds.

Seville Orange Marmalade

(Illustrated opposite)

METRIC		IMPERIAL
4	Seville oranges	4
2	sweet oranges	2
1	lemon	1
2.25 litres	water	$4\frac{1}{2}$ pints
1.75 kg	preserving sugar, warmed	4 lb

For a richer colour and flavour, replace up to a quarter of the quantity of sugar in marmalade with rich soft brown sugar. Do not add too much or the set will not be quite as firm.

Halve the fruit and extract the juice and pips. Peel the fruit and shred the peel to the required thickness. Tie the pips in a muslin bag and place in a saucepan with the peel, juice and water. Bring to the boil and simmer gently for about 2 hours until the peel is tender.

Remove the bag of pips, squeeze to remove any liquid. Stir in warmed sugar, clip a sugar thermometer to the pan and boil rapidly to 106 c/222 f. (If not using a thermometer, place a little of the marmalade on a cold saucer. The surface should pucker slightly when touched.) Leave to stand for half an hour. Stir and turn into warm sterilised jars. Label. (It will keep for about 1 year.) **Makes 2.25–2.75 kg (5–6 lb).**

Pear, Pineapple and Lemon Jam

METRIC		IMPERIAL
1 kg	fresh pineapple	2 lb
1 kg	pears	2 lb
3	lemons, juice only	3
1.75 kg	preserving sugar, warmed	4 lb

Peel the pineapple, remove the hard core and chop the flesh roughly. Peel, core and slice the pears. Put both fruits into a saucepan and heat gently until the juices appear and the fruit starts to soften. Simmer for 15 minutes until the pineapple is soft then add the lemon juice and warmed sugar. Stir until sugar is dissolved. Clip a sugar thermometer to the pan and boil to 104 c/220 f. (If not using a thermometer, place a little jam on a cold saucer. The surface should pucker slightly when touched.) Pour into warm sterilised 450-g (1-lb) jars, cover, seal and label. (It will keep for about 1 year.) **Makes 4–6 jars.**

Clockwise from top left: Rhubarb and Fig Jam (page 105), Seville Orange Marmalade and Clementines in Brandy (page 105)

Index